SELECTED LATER POEMS

for Sue

Selected Later Poems

PETER FINCH

seren

seren is the book imprint of
Poetry Wales Press Ltd.
57 Nolton Street, Bridgend, Wales, CF31 3AE
www.seren-books.com

ISBN 987-1-85411-440-2

A CIP record for this title is available from the British Library.

The publisher acknowledges the financial assistance of the Welsh Books
Council.

Cover image: Peter Finch at the Merlin, Budapest.

Printed in Hoefler by CPD Wales, Ebbw Vale

CONTENTS

from Food

from MAKE (1990)

MAKE

Can do this with any condition head
Can crack it with most
Can get a little if
Can splice ends fast when
Can stick it having
Can turn out even
Can harden
Can screw

Can
Can bend
Can lean upright
but

falls over
      (wind)

2:45 pm WARMING

Thermostat clicks, calls for heat.

Rain crackles like bracken burning.

Two minor poets sold
exchange a third
spine cracked or garbage.

Integrity eclipsed.
What's important is size.

OPPORTUNITIES

How many are
there? Half of them
gone   more. Like
anti-freeze weakened out through
an untight screw a smudge, a
residue. A few things I like
but it's mostly habit. I wrote them out in
order once on a scrap of paper   put it
out for the milkman by mistake   wonder what
he made of
        one pint only
        bks
        running
        women
        climbing
        winning
not real enough anyway. I keep getting
this work ethic in the back of the
throat and have to clean things or
write them down   deadheaded
six roses   scratched the grease
out the back of the bath   recased the guitar
Big Bill Broonzy didn't even play one
until he was 40. I think.

PIANO

piano   plinkaplonk   back of
the till   dot matrix blur
you can't read a book with a cone of
fast chips but try sliding paperbacks
into wellingtons or just walking through
the door   you get
dogs man on a bike once   light
sucks the red out of the spines until they
look the colour of raw crabmeat   lost three
copies of J.H. Prynne and sold none
best trade is a postcard with a picture of
a quiet sheep   dusk   sun ceases to
clone itself   weeds
a foot high at the wall edge
shall I run up the road
after the bearded man in the loose trousers or
shall I stay here and garden?
phone goes   turn the piano down

THE BEST GESTURE

He seems to think that his time
is overfull and that he needs to stop now and then.
But maybe this is just an excuse not
to do something else. It's not being lazy for its own sake
but a sign that he doesn't like
starting. It's a huge push, isn't it, getting
onto the bike in your waterproofs and with
all your bags and parcels strung around you.
When it goes it goes, it's starting. He slips
back a bit in to whatever he did last
night or thought he did. So long as
he knows the names of everything around
him he's okay. There's a storm
coming up outside in the pattern of
storms. Colder, lots of litter up
in arbitrary spirals, increasing wind.
It's a hard time to get a grip onto anything especially
when it changes. Perhaps his best
gesture would be to start. But he won't do
that, will he, not yet

RUNNING A READING

The street rucks up with raging
cars   slam   radios   next
door they thump cement from
a bucket   familiar
territory.   I ask the readers
if all this distracts   they answer slowly
like I was deaf   no.
Out of the window are huge, four-
engined seagulls   diving.
I reckon starting 15 minutes a
crack   they all do 40
images like butter   blunt   heads
clogged with garble   fog   the last
piece is in numbered slabs
enormous   the audience
will it   but it won't go
sways   like wool
unravelling   applause drifts
a cloud of slow mosquitoes.
I leave now   running   silence
ah silence   glorious   but when I get there
the pub is closed.

LETTER

We apologise   no credit
on behalf of delay in
(copy) two copies
screen copy
ledger
trade manager will issue a
rectify but
remaining on your account.
May I take this opportunity
of wishing you the compliments
of the season.

MUSIC

1.

I asked a lot about it
Did it?
Would it mount up?
Could I translate it?
I thought of it like
batteries you could recharge.
Hear another
fills up.
Everyone did it.
Air in the lungs.
You picked your own if
there were problems. Streak it.
Make it. If you couldn't you hummed.

2.

The ease with which some
had pieces of skin formed.
The breath cut-off.
The information at the beginning.
The distortion of space, the
bending of clarity into a
stubborn fit.
The regular clang not the smooth.
The loop. The scratch.
The ecstasy.

3.

Rain.
Sun warp.

Hot water ashtray.
Two story controlled descent.
Sat on.
Scrape.
Like a tooth necklace.

4.

To get the echo here
we had the door at the
rear open and the sound
going down two flights before
bouncing back up.
It was like singing in
a changing room.

5.

love   home   cruel   home   christmas
twist   sunday   date   sea
teen-angel   new orleans   man   love
dance   young   summer   love   ding-a
-ling   apache   love   world   poetry   exodus
heart   tonight   love   kangaroo
north   love   alaska   night   devil
angel   walk   run   baby   midnight
boogie   boll   weevil   stranger   shore
love   twist   quarter   river
jack   pony   love   romeo   rebound
mountain   love   sue   stomp   heart
tonight   twist   tonight   twist
tonight   twist   tonight   twist
tonight

we could do this

we could do this again and again
speaker leads, philips plugs
bolt shaking
spray of desire
put my hand in down there
when it's warm

paper   wonderful   teen   new   old
true   love   itsy   bitsy   teenie
weenie   yellow   banjo   handy   handy   good
wonderful   sweet sentimental   wooden
runnin'   lonely   rubber
babysitin'   moody   mint   cruel
bad   peppermint   runaround
right   tonight   tonight   tonight
tonight   tonight   tonight
yes   tonight

hum what you can remember
tap your steel comb on the fireguard
to fill in the rest

stomp boogie   please   woogie
twist mr postman   twist

6.

Christened Ernest Evans he derived the stage name Chubby Checker
from that of pianist and hit maker Fats Domino. No 1 in USA, 18
weeks in the bestsellers list 1960 and again in 1962 making a record
stay of 36 weeks in all. Rhythm-and-blues vocalist Rockin' Little
Angel Judd born in Puducah, Kentucky, learned to play the guitar
while at high school prior to entering show business. Johnny was an
engineering draughtsman. Joe appeared at record hops, he writes his
own arrangements. While at school he took lessons on the trumpet
and became very proficient. He wrote his first song at the age of 14
and also learned to play five instruments. He sang in backgrounds on

other artists' discs after persistently asking record companies for a
test. He plays ukulele as well as singing. He has a back pocket full of
spare strings. He has a lonely room. He can do the watusi. In 1960 he
bought a mojo from a hustler and has never looked back

> overnite I was layin down
> I heard moma n popa talkin
> I heard popa tell moma
> let that boy boogie woogie
> it's in him an
> it gotta come out.
> An I felt so good
> went on an boogie just the same.

> He's a rock and roll cowboy
> with jumping beans inside his jeans.

7.

> The legends and excuses.
> Flat matchwood
> trucked   warped
> No way the fingerboard.
> Blew a suck it. Bottle end. Slide it.
> Shout and yodel.
> Cheap excesses.
> Three day non-stop dances.
> How long can you shout without a microphone?
> How many people can sit on a?
> How much sweat when?
> Who gains if you?
> How can the?
> Whose pocket do you?
> How fats will the?
> How much can?
> How often will?

How much will?
How often can?
how much   how often
how often   how often
how many   how much
how can   how much
how often   how can
can can   often often
this is the way to do it
this is the way to do it
once you're there it rolls
who cares about how it sounds.

JOURNAL

July 87: I've got the fan spinning and above
its noise you can hear planes
echoing because of the lack of cloud. In the
lane they're unloading beer crates and
you can make out the voices of the workmen
but not precisely what they say. As part of the
great way none of this is really important I suppose
but it's a direction; the problem
is the weight of past experience
brimming up around me in a muscular froth.
There is a sound of someone lashing
metal with a bamboo stake and in
the distance a train clattering.
The choices are enormous. I've yet to decide.
I listen to them all.

Ultimately the shi syndrome has to be eased
and this is done by simply forgetting. The entire
library falls apart after 10 years anyway
pages brown   cracking sounds as you
open the covers. The knowledge just stops dead;
doesn't pass on.

Inside the spinning fan are at least
three smaller sounds:
    electric hum
    air movement
    mechanical vibration
and that last itself made of
bits. I try to quieten it all by
balancing the device on a soft
surface. I hold the fan up on the palm of my
hand like you do with an indoor TV aerial
when the picture fails and with as much success.
The air goes up and across the ceiling
and the lightshade sways.

Memory
a gap in the index between
Melancholy and
Meridians
faded out like red wallpaper   turned pink
each event pared into tight images
told to friends   scratched in notebooks
shaky photographs   hair clippings
bits of cloth   marks of heads on walls.

Entry for 6 June, 1967: Warm. Smell of joss sticks, people waving sparklers, things that flash and glow in the dark. At the Roundhouse Arthur Brown and his Famous Flames, rear doors to the railway open, winos up from the tracks, the iron distance running behind them into the night. Arthur Brown has his hat on fire and these red-faced failures are cheering. For a time it seems like the decade really works.

When Kerouac died nobody told me, why should they, if they put it on the news I didn't hear. Nobody broadcast it in Boots record dept like they did when Elvis went. No fans clustered shaking their heads over RCA record sleeves. Pan Books didn't bother, just let him carry on, fading out of print, slipping off into the past. I found out about it in casual conversation months later and didn't want to believe. It was hot. Memory exaggerates.

There is balance in everything. The tennis ball bounces in smaller arcs ever smaller until movement becomes a slow roll and the yellow rubber slides under the leaves at the edge of the grass. Friction ceases. The players hunt but don't find it. They may open a new tube and restart but essentially it's still the same game.

Gate of the spirit
Great shrine
Inner gateway
Complete bone
Wind screen
Storehouse of earth
Clash of the jaws
Bright eyes
Four whites

Fragrant meeting
Lesser marsh
Big monument
Sustaining centre
Axis of heaven
Central pole
Bubbling spring
Vessel of conception
Centre of man

Q: Which is most important?
A: Breath

Breath everytime

In the car park there is grass up through the tarmac. A stout ryegrass looping over where it's been sprayed but still not quite dead. I must have been here thousands of times in 13 years but I leave no trace. If I try maybe I can encode something in written imagery, *like this,* but the significance is little. Who else has moved through this matrix? Why do I need to know?

The street repeats itself each year, subtle changes like a blue sky crossed by cloud always moving ever different always the same. Stringer is done up like a red indian scout, feathers, beads, leather boots, for 10p he'll paint your face how he thinks real indians do. It makes more money than writing. I smile at him but he can't remember me. It's been 20 years anyway since he was last here with his Burroughs-like obsession with cut text and his belief that poetry would change the world. I can't be bothered to explain what's happened in all the time that lies between us. That early boldness all turned to failure. He takes a coin and starts a fresh customer. I walk on.

Perhaps this takes the soul of it
writing it down
I fill my lungs to maximum capacity
sucking in air until my diaphragm
sinks and that pulse of charged
tension makes itself felt

this is the way without thought
but not without knowledge

I cannot bear the idea of a great emptiness
I fear vacuity

I stand next to the fan
and listen to the air mingle with the whirling.
It's there.
This way I know I'm still safe.

ISLAND

You are at the edge of a square lake. In the centre is a square island. You have three planks of wood, none of which are quite long enough to reach across fully from shore to shore. How do you get across?

1. Description of the top of the brain as a dried peat bog or cutaway section across a volcano showing fault lines. There is pain somewhere off below it, the result of stress or more likely drink. Usually this takes a good 18 hours to filter up.

2. Contraction of the above sent to a famous poetry magazine and returned with a note saying they understood, the editor had been in a similar situation many times himself and the line about "the hangover like a fog of frozen rain" seemed to pin-point it. The note stopped then as if there should have been another sentence saying "we've taken a Xerox and will use it in our next issue". Even held the thing up to the light to see if their typer had gone on with its ribbon slipped. Tried floating a plank and then standing on it. Didn't work.

3. Clark Coolidge Solution Passage has it "Where the wires cross the street / the lacing of a shoe / eye meets middle / and the gulls gel" which isn't a jumping point. Well known poet I once knew would have revamped this under his own name did this often, continued even after being caught out for reassembling John Clare into contemporary Anglo-Welsh verse patterns. Why should he worry so long as it was only one or two that found him out? He hadn't discovered cut-up or collage. I supposed being modern they didn't appeal but they've been a boon to a large range of young bucks keen to cut the avant garde with a bit of swagger and no talent. In the end it is stamina that pays. Just thinking about levitation is never good enough on its own. You have to go out there and make it happen.

4. Mark Rothko 1903-1970. From this time (1940) one senses that the artist is no longer leading his art but following it. People spend much more time with the dark canvases than any others looking vainly I suppose for a glimpse of light. This is religion. Rothko had no time for planks.

5. There are obvious parallels here with the exorcism argument. Difficulty makes the whole operation a private activity. I sit adjusting this flux of structures, patterning what I have into some kind of permanence simply in order to hold it, stop it from slipping back into the maw of dream. You could argue that this was an indulgence on my part and having accused others of the same thing I must agree that it could be right.

6. Difficulty worries me only when I consider that I have to eventually do something with it.

7. Fan clouding bird-song, neither are complicated.

8. Hide the planks in the undergrowth. Stand well back before running, there is no possibility of failure. The leap and the destination are the same thing. Go.

9. Get there.

10. If you are wet you are thinking and not doing. Try again.

From POEMS FOR GHOSTS (1991)

ROOFER

It is a day
when it rains from
when I wake
to when I stop.
The lane is like gloss artex,
the gutter full of glass,
our down-pipe swan-neck rusted,
gushing like a bust cod piece.
The noise amazes me,
dogs diving through shale,
men with sticks.
The tar fix to repair
the flat roof fails as I watch it.
Black sludge everywhere,
nothing sticks.
I ring the roofer,
cash in hand for a quick job,
no cheques.
His line is busy, engaged,
no answer, redial,
busy, dial, engaged.
Then there's a voice, crackling,
just like him.
I'm sorry, it says,
sounding furtive,
but I don't work here
and the roofer's not in.

3 AM

Startled by a crash
I wake up sweating,
thrash, condensation
as much on me as on the window.
I wipe it off in a circular motion with
the edge of the curtain like I'd told
the kids not to and look out into the
black at the empty frost.
Maybe it was the fat boy from the
flat across the back shooting his airgun
from the fire-escape and hitting
or a house collapsing
like the one last winter two streets away
where the owner had knocked out all the floors
and the ice got in like water.
In the dark I can't see.
Isn't the steelworks or the shunting yard
    closed
or the docks
    empty.
When I pull it back
from the maw of dissolving
memory it sounds
like a phantom;
ghost ships loading,
steam in the power lines,
trains arriving:
what else?
Hinkley Point is 18 miles off across the Channel.
It said 15 in last night's paper.
It's getting closer.

WE CAN SAY THAT

We speak the language. No,
We understand it. We say that.
The bricks of our houses
are thick with it.
We know all the songs
and the place names.
It's not foreign.
We flaunt our origin
in the big city
where most don't
know iaith y nefoedd
from Urdu.
We do.
Heol y Frenhines it says
and we can say that.
We are native.
We have status.
Cenedl heb iaith cenedl heb galon
until we have to handle it
in Penrhyndeudraeth or Pwllheli
where, using English slyly,
we say we're glad it isn't dead.

OUT AT THE EDGE

Pembrokeshire Coast Path in winter

The wind comes in off the sea at Nolton
filling the Mariner's car park with sand.
There are no cars.
At the tide edge a lone tripper
throws a pebble through the drizzle.
I watch, dripping, with two ducks
and a chicken,
from the bottom of a barren hedge.
When I climb the track
towards Druidstone I leave bootmarks
like fossils in the fluid mud.
Why do it?
Beauty, light, passion.
Who knows.
I get the feeling that if there is
an edge to this world then it is here.
From the headland I stare out at America
but don't see it.
Mist, distance, earth's curvature,
or maybe it just isn't there.

MOUNTAINS: SHEEP

I am halfway to the summit
and it starts to rain.
I am surrounded by sheep.
Behind me like bunting
strung over the fences
of five counties
are parts of their fleece.

Amid this wool, grease, suint,
urine, dung, burs, seeds, twigs,
sand, soil, dip and salve
are the bones of their faces
impassively arrayed.

You can talk to them and
they'll answer. I once held
a flock with Schwitter's
Ursonata. Recognising
quality they stayed.

They outnumber us.
Standing shank to shank
they would fill Zanzibar,
and still leave
the hills unscathed.

At the top where they cluster
the rain is a tight grey.
The outcrops run with graffiti
genitalia enormously displayed

In the sheep this raises
no passion. While I seethe
they stand and shit.

When I go
they stay.

HUNTING WHITAKERS FOR THE ANSWER TO POETRY

How To Be A Gifted Parent
How To Be Born Again
How To Be Decadent
How To Be Poor
How To Be Top
How To Be Your Cat's Best Friend
How To Boil An Egg
How To Beat Fatigue
How To Buy An IBM PC
How To Catch Tiddlers
How To Cheat At Cooking
How To Cope With Insomnia
How To Do Things With Words
How To Draw
How To Drive Your Man Wild In Bed
How To Flatten Your Stomach
        Get Out Of The Bath
        Get Pregnant
How To Get Rid Of Your Double Chin
How To Lie With Statistics
        Live With A Working Wife
How To Restore And Repair Practically Anything
How To Save Your Life
How To Seduce Any Man In The Zodiac
        Shoot An Amateur
        Solve Chemistry Problems
        Stop A Train With One Finger
How To Stop The Phone Ringing
        Dominate Your Readers
        Drown In A Saucer Of Water
        Succeed Every Time
How To Appear In *Poetry Wales*
How To Store Great Speeches In Bottles
        Echo Death

Ride Boxcars
Meditate, Mix, Mould
Repeat
Use Voice As A Device
Disintegrate, Reiterate
Cock An Ear To The Ground
How To Vibrate, Rotate, Levitate
    Understand 246 Different Words For Rain
    Know 300 Sheep By Their Skull Shape
How To Use Your Tongue Like A Plane

Brmm Brmm
It's easy

How To Be Like Gunn
               Clampitt
               Larkin
               Motion
               Kinnell
How To Be Like Raine
How To Sound Like Hughes
    Deal With Death
    Write Like Plath
    Drink Like Tripp
How To Jump Like Hart Crane
What you do is you
steal from those no longer with us,
change bits so
it doesn't sound the same.
Sit in your room and
work out why the past has little
to teach you.
What you do know
you don't understand anyway.

Do you know about fog?
Poetry is best in fog.
Mis-spell, shuffle, sweat.
Turn on the typer
open up a vein.

LANGUAGE

Outside the bookshop
still raining.
Dark grey right up the street.
Woman at the desk
like Joan Collins
you can see the age
creeping up out
of the dress, hanging
around the throat like crepe.

Gang of skinheads
at the till buying
learn-in-a-day Welsh course.
Isn't possible.
In Gwynedd no one even
acknowledges you until you've
done ten years –
bending the adenoids,
swallowing syllables,
keeping the home fires
going.

Joan Collins eventually
chooses a 1987 Welsh diary,
reduced this August to 5p for a quick sale.
The path to satori is
littered with boulders,
But on these hills they all look like sheep.

Why are they doing it? Learning
Welsh in the council estate south.

I check the guest
armchair which is angled
specifically to allow cash

to roll back from its occupants'
pockets and into the waiting seam.
One pound and one pence.
I check off the
sitters this week:
Dafydd Wyllt
Rajiv Gandhi
The rep from Thames and Hudson
My mother on a fleeting visit
George Willoughby
Cary Archard

How much fantasy is there in this?
Couldn't be Rajiv, he has no pockets
and I invented George Willoughby
to fatten out the list.

The skinheads are now
on the stairs practising
sher my you wanker
dai yown dee olch
sit bloody chi fart punch.
When I get back to
the shelves I
spot a few significant
gaps in the art section
and note that all the videos are
unaccountably gone. At such a juncture
others might have
locked themselves in the
bog with the giant nobert
graffitied on the door
and sweated cockles
about what to do next.
But not me,
I knew.
No bloody point in

reporting it
no one cares.
Up onto one
leg like a golden rooster
and calmly check
for swear words
in the *Collins-Spurell Modern English-Welsh Dictionary.*

Relief by expletive.
Page 393: *Flip* – verb.
In Welsh – *Fflipio.*

Doesn't work. No strength.
Reality has again been
tampered with.
I put the book back
in the history section.
A grey sea full of rocks.
Through the windows are
the sounds of the city
dampened by rain.

KIPPER ON THE LIPS

O Cod,
I feel a right prawn.
Try to kipper outside the cinema.
Obviously the wrong plaice.
Welcoming bream turns into a foul mackerel,
next minnow she's slapping my face.
I'm amazed.
What a dolphin to do.
Have I got halibutosis? A stickle back?
Squid in my trousers? No way.
I'm just a flash haddock after her turbots.
Look at this conger eel, I say.
But she's into big bivalves
and long-distance gurnards,
so I flounder,
What a elver time to distrust
your encrustation.
The sea trout's out, I'm a failure.
She goes off with a sperm whale.
I light up a bloater.

DEAD END

At the bottom of the cupboard a cake tin
decorated with a print of an embroidered horse.
Inside an unused diary for '72,
a tin of snuff, cigarette lighters,
golfball, a trick ring, flints,
an opened packet of mignonette seeds
with a trace of mud along the top.

The seeds went into a plot I'd cleared.
No idea about horticulture, cut the old tea roses
down with a hacksaw, left the roots in.
Brown clay like a building site,
all hoof prints, rucks and cracks.
The dead cat came half back up
it's black head knocked sideways by a
neighbour backing his car;
too much beer. Never said.
The owners suspected me, the infidel.
Accusations and weeping around the doorway got us nowhere.
They thought television a weapon of the devil,
refused me permission to staple my aerial co-axial
across their window-frame. They imagined
this way they could make me pure,
Jesus, all I did was chuck their
tracts back at them. Nothing more.

I threw the mignonettes into dips scooped
in the orange hardback with a dessert spoon.
No concept of germination or knowledge of how
deep these things ought to lay. Leave it to chance,
hope for rain. Sat on the step with a flagon of
homebrew, task done, stared at the fence
and the bushes and the sky beyond.
Art is not stealth;
it leaps out at you.
Too much Whitman and Blake
makes you blind.

No one had cleared the yard
in living memory.
Ragwort sprouting through
cracked tarmac,
bramble,
ivy tangled through garbage
pink campion in a rolling haze.

reasons for drinking:

a) art
b) oblivion

Can't improve it.

Pulled up a plant, threw it back.

Went into the flat and lay on the settee.
Looked at the message written on
the wallpaper above the firegrate:
"Thanks for the drink, love JT."
A poet who could do it.
When I complained he said
scrape it off and sell it.

Dead now. Message painted out.
Surplus seeds back in the packet,
lid on top.

The past is all echo,
stop listening.

Never saw any flowers,
nothing came up.

LITTLE MAG

Spend three hours
addressing envelopes.
Bic exhausted.
Towards the finish
the hand finds itself
totally unable to complete the
tight circle of a letter o.

The mags go out like ack-ack.

In exchange I get misprints
highlighted, protest, left topher
off his name, no comma, word missing,
poems, two renewals, one cancellation,
a shaky essay on the work
of someone I've never heard of,
a pair of sandals, a dead fish.

At the Post Office I have a
deal where they stick the stamps
and I pay,
"Too much bad language,"
says the supervisor with a hat,
speaking to me as
if I were a Martian.
"We have women here."
I make a note.

In the pub I drink
to wash it all out of me
but the landlord's got
a new one can't wait.
It comes at me across the pump
handles like a singing telegram.
Crap can't tell him.
Have another pint, I smile.
Pretty full, I say.

Tomorrow, the library,
abuse in the bookstores,
rain.
A bag of post like a
sack of kippers.

Dear Editor,
I enclose 38 poems about love.
My friends say these
are better than anything
else they've read.
I would like to buy your
magazine please send a
free copy.
I will pay for one
when I'm in it.

I enclose
Here are
I am sending
Please find
I submit
Could you
Will you
Please
It is important that
I hope
I must
I have to
I'm the best
I don't bother usually
but these poems of mine are
so well put together that I
read them twice after
writing them.

You are the way
You are the path
You are the light
You are the last beacon
in this verbal wilderness.

I have faith.
Help me.

But I cannot.
Poetry is short on miracles.
I send a rejection.

Instead.

DUTCH

He didn't have enough energy. He'd been talking all morning about Holland and how in the golden age of his youth friends from the Translation Foundation had come to visit in their Dutch car like a snail with deck-chairs. The tale had centered on how the car wouldn't climb hills with a full load because it was used to flat polders. Someone told the joke about how Italian cars wouldn't start in the mornings here because they missed the sun. He got onto the Dutch attitude to language and everyone said it was wonderful how they all seemed to speak English. The Translation Foundation had been a soft touch - they had paid for him to publish small books by a whole series of clever Dutch modernists who would otherwise never have appeared anywhere but in their own country. At the time it had made him feel important, part of the great European tradition. No one bought the books, of course, but the reviews had been good. He told everyone of what he'd done and, even now, decades later, people were still impressed.

He had possessed the strength then. He could think about just one thing all day. Now he found it hard to manage five minutes. He didn't read. Television advertisements with their 60s r'n'b soundtracks and tight, miniature storylines were pretty much all he could cope with. He liked to sit in his arm chair, surfing channels with the remote and fiddling about with the levels of brightness, contrast and colour.

Towns in Holland beginning with H

Heerenveen
Hoogeveen
Haarlem
Hellendoorn
Hertogenbosch
Hippolytushoef
Heemstede

They all seemed to.

He couldn't remember where his translator friends had come from. Hoek van Holland? The men had just been like him but the women had been huge. One of them could lift paving slabs single-handed. They all wore Netherlandisch Levis and as they travelled about - museum, pub, Wentlooge Levels to inspect our own drained flatland - they hummed songs by the Rolling Stones.

Symptoms of fatigue:

a) Increase in the basal pulse rate (monitored before getting out of bed). He would think himself into the heart, put his mental hands onto the valves and muscles and try to slow it down. He'd clear his head. Think of nothing. Blackness. Poems trying to get in at the sides. He'd shoot them down.

b) Increased infections (colds, sore throat, lip sores, etc.). Reasons for not thinking about writing at all.

c) Dizziness on standing up quickly. Old man symptom. You'd see them all over the place, old men, holding onto walls, hatstands, the sides of urinals. Now him. If you want to improve then practise a lot but do it right. He stood badly. Always had. He'd been doing it for so long that he was now an expert.

d) Waking up very early in the morning. Engage in writing. Throw the results away.

e) Chronic tiredness and lack of progression. All his works came back. He had a desk full of rejection. He told the translators that people often didn't know what to make of him. Established literary figures would stop just short of rudeness. He was never included in anything. The translators suggested he give himself a Dutch persona; masquerade his works as translations from the low-land originals. He was weird enough. No one would guess.

f) Unusual irritability. Pretty easy, expected of an artist. Irascible old rogue, grumpy bastard, that writer over there, the miserable bugger, all that.

In the pub they arm wrestled for halves of cider. He beat everyone except the women. It was a natural talent. He'd grown strong bicycling, walking, rock climbing. He didn't think about it. "Hills," he told them, "the answer to everything." They shook their heads. One of them showed him a contour map of the Netherlands. Not a bump in sight. The shape of their country reminded him of a regimental flag worn to tatters in battle. He nodded his head.

He knew nothing at all about Dutch literature. He couldn't name one figure. He didn't immediately confess this ignorance but it soon became obvious. The translators asked his advice about the market, who had done well, what sort of thing they studied in the universities and he bluffed. They told him things about the literary scene in Holland, which surprised him. Netherlandisch William Burroughs cutting canal drug novels into telephone directories, Dutch super surrealist sound poets, literary performers who chanted into arrays of brass tubing, detective writers with a tradition of fish mysteries, modernist critics hated by the European establishment, minimalists, misogynists, imagists, post-Poundian perambulators, Martians, dud mathematicians, epilogists, eulogists, rock revivalists, soap commercial trad bands, white bicycles, inflators, bigheads, literary bastards and plagiarizers. It sounded a wonderful place. What they told him was mostly invention but he wasn't to know.

References to Holland in:

Graham Swift's *Shuttlecock*. A Psychological thriller. "Excellent, profound and very odd" - *London Review of Books*. None.

The Oxford Book of Aphorisms - Archbishop Whateley's Apophthegm of 1864 reads "To know your ruling passion, examine your Dutchman in the air." This is probably a misprint.

The Companion To Dutch Literature recommends *The Merchant of Amsterdam, Much Ado About Netherlanders, A Bend In The Dutchman, La belle Hollander Sans Merci,* and *The Merry Wives of Wassenaar.* Most other works with a Dutch flavour are regarded as either insulting or as fakes.

In Graham Creeley's novel *A Fastness For Europe,* Holland is referred to as a "scraped peat bog full of indolent translators" and its literature as "a dull mirror of continental conservatism". Creeley worked for years as a river engineer re-aligning Dutch watercourses as the Zeider Zee turned from liquid into land. His speciality at that time was the limerick. There is reference in *The Encyclopaedia Netherlandiae* to his collapse from fatigue while attempting a marathon along frozen canals during the 50s. His *Low Countries Be Buggered* trilogy dates from this period.

Roget's *Thesaurus* has Dutch stone, Dutch barns, Dutch caps, Dutch treats, Dutch uncles, Dutch gin, going Dutch, double Dutch, my old Dutch, out for a Dutch, a Dutch is as good as a wink, and a Hollander in time saves nine.

His Dutch friends would spend the mornings translating texts, ringing up publishers on his phone, arranging meetings. He remembered especially how the big women would look at him. He never did anything about it although he later always claimed that he had. Tales of size were more impressive in the way wide-screen cinema is. Longer lasting like large apples. He told the tale about sitting in the filing cabinet drawer and the one about the vacuum cleaner and the airing cupboard. He even embellished things by recounting another from a different context where the girl had taken a photocopy of her bum by sitting on the glass screen as the machine moved her back and fore. Dutch days, quite the best.

No one asked him how he'd managed it with no energy. The question didn't arise, everyone thought he was a bit of a lad. Someone bought another round and emboldened he had a pint this time. Could he name any Dutch literary figures today? He scratched his nose for a moment and looked out of the window and the slowly rising landscape. Not a hope.

EX-SMOKES MAN WRITES EPIC

eleven paragraphs on persuasion

1. Illusions

Breathe in. Place hot end in mouth. Close lips tightly. Blow.
Smoke pours out through filter.

Brown fingertips, nicotine traces.
This is the mark of a man.

Breathe through handkerchief.
Look at the stain.

Cigarette in ear.

Double smoke rings through nostrils.

Move cigarette from nose
to mouth without using hands.

2. Exotica

Three cigarettes in mouth simultaneously.

Break wind. Light gas with glowing
stub held close to trousers.

3. Art

Blue Book, Passing Cloud, Gold Flake,
Three Tuns, Black Cat, Senior Service,
Capt to Cairo, Domino,
ten pack, Van Gough, tan mackintosh,
cool posture, hard type, pure hype.

4. Pain

Rip skin off lower lip with Woodbine.

Grip slips down shaft stuck to mouth by
lip blood. Burn fingertips.

Lighted end of cheap French fag falls out
and enters shoe.

King-size concertinerd into face by door slam.
Chest set alight by falling debris.

Benson and Hedges used for gesture in cinema
sets light to lacquered beehive of woman sitting in front of you.
Use of aerosol to subdue flame only makes matters worse.
Conflagration finally fire-hosed by manager wearing dinner suit.
Tell-tale dibbies found beneath your seat.
Thrown out for being under age.

5. Vandalism

Brown stain on ceiling over bed.

Brown stain on walls in living-room.

Brown stain on toilet cistern.

Burn marks on dressing table.

Burn marks on kitchen shelf.

Burn marks on lid of record player.

Hole in carpet.

Singe marks on ties, shirts, lapels, sandwiches.

I once found a fag-end in a meat pastie
and a bit of cork-tip in a tin of corned beef.

ha ha
ho ho.

6. Health

Cure? cough I don't cough care cough enough
can't be cough easy cough cough
cough cough can cough it?
I ought cough to cough
shit cough cough stop cough
cough cough
cough.

7. Politics

But then again why should I?

8. Sociology

My grandfather lived to be 80.

9. Religion

If God hadn't wanted us to smoke
he wouldn't have given us lungs.

10. Sex

Panatela owner seeks ashtray.
No risk – built-in filter.

11. Final Appeal

Ladies and Gentlemen,
consider the following:

    a) T.S.Eliot smoked a pipe.
    b) Cowboy Copas could roll a cheroot with one hand
       while sitting on a horse.

Both are dead,
or so I'm told.
I rest my case.

HILLS

Just an ordinary man of the bald Welsh hills,
docking sheep, penning a gap of cloud.
Just a bald man of the ordinary hills,
Welsh sheep gaps, docking pens, cloud shrouds.
Just a man, ordinary, Welsh doctor, pen weaver
cloud gap, sheep sailor, hills.
Just a sharp shard, hill weaver, bald sheep,
pilot pen rider, gap doctor, cloud.
Just a shop, sheer hill weaver, slate,
balder, cock gap, pen and Welsh rider,
Just slate shop, hill balder, cocking,
shop gap. Welsh man, cloud pen.
Just shops, slate, cocks, bald sheep,
Welsh idea, gutteral hills, ordinary cloud.
Just grass gap, bald gap, garp grap,
grap shot, sheep slate, gap grap.
garp gap
gop gap
sharp grap shop shap
sheep sugar sha
shower shope sheep
shear shoe slap sap
grasp gap gosp gap
grip gap grasp gap
guest gap grat gap
gwint gap grog gap
growd gap gost gap
gap gap gwin gap
gap gop gwell gap
gap gop gap gap
gap gap gap gap
gap gap gorp gap
gap gap gap gap
gap gap gap gap
gap gap gap gap
gap gap gap gap
gap gap gap

immigrant slate mirth grot gap
bald grass, rock gap, rumble easy,
old gold gap, non-essential waste gap,
rock docker, slow slate gap, empty rocker,
rate payer, waste gap, cloud hater,
grasper balder, pay my money, dead,
trout shout, slate waste, language nobody
uses, bald sounds, sends, no one pens,
fire gap, failed gasps,
dock waste, holiday grey gap,
hounds, homes, plus fours, grip sheep,
four-wheeled Rover: Why not? Soft price,
grown gravel, sais

The problem gaps, ordinary television,
nationalist garbage, insulting ignorance,
shot sheep, invited bald interference,
don't need real sheep where we are,
sheepless, sheepless, Welsh as you are, still,
no gasps, gogs or gaps for us,
no,
point our aerials at the Mendip Hills.

FORM

1. I would describe my cultural and ethnic
   origin as being of:

   > European origin (including British)
   > African origin
   > Asian origin
   > Other – please state which: *Martian*

2. Have you any tendencies? YES/NO

3. Remedial teaching. Is this
   YES/NO. Did you know
   of this before? Could/Could* (*delete one)
   Subject to change in local educational
   provision

4. Have you suffered from any of the following:

   > epilepsy
   > gum disorder
   > mental handicap
   > sensory deprivation
   > age-linked handicap
   > chest fantasy
   > heart condition

5. who ist pur effe
   rentor ure ment roger
   iss iss ap are ap bum

6. signed (space) signature not essential

7. Complete forms as soon as possible
   Delay will not affect although it may.
   Assess adequately effectiveness house
   boat.

8. wind channelled between two tall buildings
   screw paper up close to microphone it sounds
   like houses burning. city hall chime 4.30
   ricochet. slip in the bottom of the
   envelope says packer 46.

9. Put in the bin and go home.

WALES FOR AMERICANS

A piece made from actual headlines found in various monthly newspapers published in north America for the ex-patriot Welsh.

Hi Ho it's Mari Lwyd
Wyoming Valley St David's Day, February 26th
Success to the gaudy Welsh Collectors Club
Dylan Classic Bedecks Yule TV
Waukesha, Wisconsin St David's Day, February 27th
Melvin O Williams named noble of the year
   by Islam Temple Shrine, San Francisco.
   Mr Williams is a Welsh speaker.
Cape Fear St David's Day, February 28th
Tegwen N. Sacco of Smithfield, Ohio,
   says "no" to progress.
   She wants Wales kept as God planned it.
Oak Hill St David's Day, March 5th

These selections have *strenj wyrds:*
   rwyt ti'n egsajyretio
   beth ydy'r pê-off?
   rhaid i mi fynd i'r corner siop am bunch of daffs.

The perfect St David's Day gift:
   Felinfoel Welsh valley Shampoo
   made from real Welsh coconuts.

Make St David's Day last all year with
Central Ohio Continuous Leek Supply

Baltimore St David's Day, September 4th

THE 1930s BRITISH BOARD OF CENSORS SCRIPT-VETTING UNIT REPORTS

Basically the story-line you have sent for consideration is harmless. However, the Board wishes to draw your attention to the following points:

1. The riddle about the seagull is vulgar and should be omitted.

2. The second verse of the song should be changed. It may be too risqué.

3. The costumes of the young lady appear to be scanty enough to demand the bringing down of the curtain on certain venues.

4. The scenes of Daphne in cami-knickers should be deleted.

5. The penguin getting drunk must be carefully handled. If the penguin is actually drunk, this is prohibited.

6. What is a pansy? This sounds as if it might be undesirable and, if so, must come out.

7. Dialogue. The following should be deleted:
   "Blanche, I love your breasts."
   "You bitch"
   "You bastard"
   "You street walker"
   "Christ Almighty"
   and all reference to corsets.

Allowing that our advice is heeded there is no reason why your play should not go on to become a resounding success.

SEVERN ESTUARY ABC

A is a hat. Sun on my head.
B is binoculars I'm using.
C across the water. Largest concentration.
D is design. Planned.
E in Europe. Believe that.
F is mud flats, wading birds.
G for godwit, green sandpiper, grey plover.
H is heavy population, heavy water.
I'm informed. I watch TV. My hat is
Just there to stop the sun burning.
Know what does it?
L is little suns in bottles. Heat.
M is the mighty atom.
N for no trouble in Oldbury, Hinkley Point, Berkley.
Old stuff, I know. They're not sure.
P soup of a public explanation.
Quantity before quality. The fuel of the future.
R is rich someone's salting somewhere. There's always someone.
Severn seeped solid. Sold down the river.
T is truth. Piece of fiction.
Ah yes.
U is understanding. It's safe.
V is very safe. Formation of ducks. Skinhead. Thatcher.
We buy it.
X marks the spot. The insidious ingress. The cancer.
Why don't we do something?
Z is the sound of us listening.

From THE SPE ELL (1995)

THE DEMONS PROJECT

The Demons Project was a commission from Swansea UK Year of Literature and Writing, 1995, for poet Peter Finch and artists Mags Harries to build a demon trap. *The Spe ell* was part of Peter Finch's contribution. Demons were sought from more than 400 writers, poets and literateurs across Wales. Each was sent a stamped postcard and asked to put on it a demon they wished to be rid of. Responses were processed to form the present spell. Special mention should be made of the reservations expressed by both James Roose-Evans and Islwyn Ffowc Elis (incorporated into the text) and of Rosemary Ellen Guley's excellent source book. Demons are literate but limited. Change their names and their power dissolves. Reduce them to threes and you can sing them out of the air.

how   **i t t**   **s h d**
b e e   **dun**

t e l   t h e   e s e
t h i   n g s
        o n e   s s s

t e l   t h m   w t h
a i y   s t r   o n g
v o y   s s s

t e l   t h m   w t h
y u r   e y e
        u p p   o n n
h e v   u n n

                       g g o

w y t	t w n	c o t
g a y	l o f	a m l
e x p	l i v	f o t
d t h	n i c	o o t
s e f	r o l	t t h
p i s	t u b	n e d
f o r	a c h	p a t
g u g	c a p	f e y
w s h	o n e	v e r
t h e	t w o	o m p
a n d	m a c	b e e
b u r	l i v	p o n
m e n	x m a	r o n
l e t	p o l	r u b
t o o	m a n	c a r
d o g	f o u	p a v
y s h	m k s	t h e
r u g	c u l	d r k
p o s	m o d	c l p
t r p	w i t	h o r
i o n	j c k	u n d
p n t	a b r	l o g
t h n	w r d	p o l
q u e	t i m	t r d
g r a	w h i	a d s
b r i	m e n	w h o
v i n	t h e	w a k
d i k	p e t	o b s

i n g	r e c	e a l
a l e	u f f	a l e
o s i	u g h	n o t
r e a	h u n	o l f
a y i	s o n	a n t
o r i	h o t	o n t
o m e	o u t	e a d
e a c	o r k	o p m
c a t	f u r	a u r
i d n	o n n	c r e
s t a	i n g	e s s
h e r	b o d	o m e
p o t	r e d	e r e
n o b	c o m	d r y
p u b	e a k	t u k
b r n	t u n	e s s
a n k	a g e	p u b
m i r	o v e	s m o
j e h	v e g	e i g
w a t	u r k	a i l
g u e	f e r	w i t
p i z	e a d	d i g
v a n	p k s	t h e
a r k	p a r	c a r
a n d	h e r	n i c
j e w	w r i	b l o
o c e	c h e	i n i
k i r	j e l	f i t

```
n ' t        r r y        a b t
t h e        t d i        f e l
u l t        a b t        t h e
t i d        f e l        u l t
```

You can not exe pec peo ple too sed aiy postcard, visible to all, with their names attached, listing their demons, that is if you are serious! Perhaps it is all meant to be one Big Lark?

And what do you mean by demons? And what do you mean by a demon trap? Anyone who has experienced psychic disorders of the kind necessitating an exorcist will warn you that it is a very serious and even psychically dangerous business.

Some, of course, will believe in demons as objective realities, - fallen angels etc., while others will grasp that they are manifestations of the unconscious, what Jung called 'the shadow' side. You cannot trap such!

```
u n f        k n d        n e s
h u m        d e m        d e m
d e m        d e m        d e m
d e m        o f f        b i g
h y p        c e n        c h o
```

aaa wne wch chi fyy esg os gwelwch yn dda? Does dim bwganon/cythreuiliaid diddorol iawn, no digri iawn, yn fy mlino i. Bydd un ddiddorol gweld pa rai sy'n poeni beirdd a llenorion eraill

```
u p p       p s e       f a k
pom         b l d       d e m
f s h       p a s       c / l
d e m       d e m       b o r
o n e       p o l       l i e
l y e       l e e       l a a
```

dem mon sss reee ple ete wit wis dom. God dem
ons eud dem ons. Evl dem ons cac ode mon sss.
Div ine pow wer. Dei fid her oes. Evl. Trp
thm. Cha nge the eir nam ees.

arbuthnot
araldite
arhoolie
able bodied
abracadabra
archibald
all souls
aldebaren
alexipharmic
ambidexteruous
ancient rites

```
bum         p o e       a s s
d e l       c t r       a d s
t h i       w t h       b i g
l y e       l e e       l a a
```

dip   dip   did
ule   dee   daa
sow

          her   wee
gow   all   the
dem   sss   iss
lin   upp   ann
wee   gon   hav
too   ent   tay
nnn   thm   aaa
li   lle   bit

how   wee   gon
doo   tis

wee   gon   pay
thm   aaa   lit
boo   gee   woo
gee   now

aaa   lit   lee
bit   off   boo
gee   woo   gee
now   ann   itt
gow   lik   tis

bom   bum   bom
bom

	bom	bum
bom	bom	
		bon
bum	bum	bum
did	dle	
bum	bum	bum
ann	wee	get
goo	ann	tey
all	sta	shh
out	and	thr
oww		
don	lik	emm
blu		
		emm
boo	gee	jaz
emm	for	inn
wee	can	ony
doo	itt	wee
can	ony	boo
gee		
	inn	wun
lan	wid	dge

```
g e s
            g o w      o n n
g e s

y o o      n o w

w u n      l a n      i d
           d g e

t h e      l a n      w i d
           d g e
           o f f
           h e v
           a n n


             *


s t r      i n g      b r k
j s t      i n n      t i m


             *


d e m      d e m      o n n
a y e      a i y      e e e
a i y      a h h      a i y
a a a      a a a      a a a
a a a      a a a      a a a
a a a      a a a      a a a
```

From ANTIBODIES (1997)

BLODEUWEDD TRANSLATED

I ws bldng n t lp f bsts
Pllng stffl t m lv. I hv t scmng
tht wnds mir n t mn. Grmnts f groc
dlt n clpp n t wnk f m il.

I m starrr f mgh mlssssss
wr tghtngngngn shot my moderness appalling
nasnasmast f I hd fop on fop on me
n t rbble f stirling I list m why

I ws bllll l l ll llls
Pllng ngngn n n ng. N ng n ngngng
tht thth t t th. Gththths yt thth
dlt o oooo o o ooo o o oo

I m storrr r rrr r mssssssss
wr starlight starlight starlight
starlight starlight starlight me
god gaths stir m m starlight why

I ss sssss sssss blod oak broom meadowsweet

HISTORY

Hills are harder
Hills are retreat

Kings are bramble
Kings are rags

Rags are hard
Rags are grass

Treachery is brittle
Treachery is table

Clinging is taut
Clung is bright

Battles are bream
Battles are hollow

Bright battles are rugs
Bramble battles are grit

Proudness is warming
Proudness is hate

Kings are warm
Kings are bright

Kings are shirts
Kings are shout

Kings are hard
Kings are arses

Hills are brittle
Hills are tables

Trenches are warm
Trout is brittle

Bards are grit grass
Bards are arse tables

Bards are bright rags
Bards are warm hinges

Hanging is hollow
Hanging is finished

King is coarse
Kong is whim

Hills are washed

Bards are hope

Kings are unable

Trout is hatred

MARIGOLD HANDS

We've bn hving a lot of trouble
with youths in the village
for quite sme time.

Nothing to do to do
bn drinking they
bn drinking trouble

I am absolutely shocked

mainly boys troub trouble s

drink and vandalism and drgs.
These are the wrecked
flower beds. This is the mayor.

They have st up a yth clb
but nothing but nothing
no no congregating
none of
nobody goes.

These are the sort st
of people who wd rather
take an A level in bus
shelters.

There is nt a council
drg meeting nobody anyway.

M. Marigold hands.

july 10.95 tickhill

SHOCK OF THE NEW

How have we got this far
on foot? Long hills full of light,
towers of distrust, the music
of falling trees. When we
began it was a matter
of dealing with demons.
Some of us could not
contain our agitation
standing up in restaurants
explaining how it would be done.

These landscapes were big and real
with nowhere to hide.
I can remember the first exorcism
failed benzedrine inhalers
cough-mixture outlawed morphine
no methedrine not enough speed
reduced to 50 Pro-plus no
idea of how the bones should sit.

There were so many of us.

Ectoplasmic creations. God or bust.
The land continuously tilting.
Fields, ditches,
nodes of time,
eyelids buttressed with sand.
Did we understand it?
What did we make of the human condition?
The sense of air on the skin?

Not much.

Singing
tinsel
small lights run off
leaking batteries.
Sung.

In the foothills we discussed
these rights of passage with others.

The Americans said do said do you do
you do it. Our educated peers
outran us   already tried our methods
and abandoned. Claimed Eliot
didn't mean this. The bloody echo
of that chiming phrase. We were
outnumbered by stone throwers. We lay down.

Ages protect themselves with grease.
In the paper-mills   a bloom on the
whiteness which won't take the ink   they
own the forests   they supply the bears.
Kill them. For twenty-five years
in the streets we met with
malcontents, revolutionaries, sellers of tracts.
Peace is milk. War is acid.
But the centre always holds.

Have had it with despair,
under the bed when the doorbell rings.

Change is a ghost,
mist between rocks.

The lever, the rod, the pole, the toothpick,
the blunt sword, the bean stick,
the tyre jack, the rule,
the rose stake, the poker,
the staff, the bo stick, the jo.

Fulcrum between power and weight
no cultural change.

A gain in power is a loss in speed.
You slow as you age.

We arrive by stealth
so quiet we surprise ourselves
our madness   a profound spectre
wearing the robes of a king.
Makers not creators
noise in our ears like earth
sliding, crowds in disarray,
only occasionally a symphony
we do different things.

Do we know why we have
arrived where we have arrived?

Does anyone listen
in the great silence
of Einstein's cylinder?

Cone to ear, water funnel,
goal mouth, fishnet,
shit bucket, chicane, drip tray,
trough, gutter, lid,
canyon, egg, belt, echo box,
bag, cage liner, wipe,
sump, antimacassar, blot.

Does much matter
when it all ends.

CLATTER

1.

I love you
I keep saying oh
On the bus you
Hear me coming up
The stairs clatter
And I'm going to say
It again sorry I love you
Clatter you're embarrassed
All your friends mmmm
Why don't I just erase

2.

The stairs clatt
Love you saying oh
I keep coming up th
And I'm going to sorry
Your frien on the bus erase
All your clatter
Why don't I
Just hear me again again
I love you I love you
Why mmmmm again

3.

The love oh oh
I keep embrarrassed
All your friends clatter
On the bus love clatter
On the stairs clatter
Hear me oh oh
Sor Why don't
Embarrassed embarrassed
Embarrassed embarrassed
mmmm erase

4.

Lov lov
Cl c clatter
I'm going to
Stairs like a again fr
Stairs like a barrier suck the
Breath in and just say it
mmmm oh oh oh oh
I'm sorry I love you you
Stairs and clatter I do again
Again I'm amazed

5.

All yr your y yr your
erase erase erase
erase erase erase
erase erase erase
erase erase erase
erase erase erase
erase erase erase
erase erase erase
erase erase erase
erase erase erase

6.

Oh I'm embar mmmm
I love your clatter I am a friend
Sorry about the the stairs don't go anywhere
Why do I
Your bus your clat
Your row of shining faces ears
Why don't I
They make me red
again I cla cla clatter
I clatter again

7.

I keep saying so your
Loud clatter and shrieks
Your army of fren I don't have any
I am so erased but bolder
I swagger
Again I am on the stairs hello
I am sorry I am
You are always sorry
I am sorry I love you don't be don't be
Oh you say

8.

Your friends are gone clatter
Embarassed erase erased
Hear me coming com I
Again I love you oh oh
Again I clatter
I am not sorry I love you
I am not era erase
Mmmm you say oh you love me
Maybe this time this time
No clatter won't be erased

9.

Bus is love oh
B bus breast coming up the stairs
Your friends r erase
I keep saying I keep saying I keep saying
Clatter if you love me I say
All your friends on the stairs
Cheering hooray oh
I love you I love you I keep clattering
Mmmm you too now not now em embarassed
Love and clatter it's okay it's okay it's okay.

SALES CONFERENCE

moving the price up it's half a price the
barrier at ninety-five he's I see not possible

the shift they ninety-nine half the how on
the trend barrier under it she'll upsell will

the rigid lift perfect sold half the run run-on
over-stickered at ninety-five she'll fly said she'll run

the running spill barrier analysis half the content we're
over-peeled half cross-sold he's hand standing can

moving under half-cut limbo limbo undo limbo
ninety-nine stick cross limbo half a can half a can

sold anyway unstick trend re-pallet lumber
dump-bin limbo he's cross cut flat-standing

he can no price can any barrier can do it
shift cross-stuck can could can can can can done

WET SINGERS

Water Jones
Blind Wet Jenkins
Bog Stitchwort Owen
The Waterstones
Foam Baby
West Glamorgan Pipe Choral
Crow Edward Rainfall
Damp Diddley Davies
The Shower Kings Oh Such Piping Hot Harmony
Tin Bath Malcolm (gtr)
The Physicians of Myddfai
Thomas The Tank Engine

YOUNG

Now as I was young and believe me
I was young enough young
I was lilting
I was once rich and young I
knew how much myself I was
spinning so passionate so help me
full of wanting   make a mark my
mark not a borrowed mark   passion alone
is not enough   got to cutting call it mine
but this generation bucks   I tell
them all told a lot of heydays
without ears   hummed myself
blank eyes   disabilities and guesses
no history hovering how
hung among fastmen and pill benders
hurled among fishmongers and pall bearers
hoisted among Finnegan and big Portnoy
hoorayed among fibrillators and Pontneddfechan unbenders
homberged among Humbert and hollow horses
hoomed along humming and hummed honking
young humming not hissing not whistling
humming humming not thinking
now I was young and believe me often
I was young and I was often I was always
I was full of new noises and big mouths singing

Why is it not like it should?
Why can't it be shining?
Why if it is, is it so little?
Why isn't it young, always young?
Why is it rich and uneasily easy?
Why does it never tell us it knows?
Why does it stutter coming?
Why can't it come fresh young, and not like paper?
Why is it all through me, dying?

item: Satriani Hendrix cloak

item: Ashbery Stevens   Ashbery Stevens
        Ashbery Stevens   Ashbery Stevens

item: we decide we do do we?
        or do we look it up?

item: (i*-!*=+@@
            unreadable - overtaken
        by a visible universe like a
        trouser leg)

item: Youngblood, Young Bones, Mighty Joe Young

What do the young want bones and my maybe thinking maybe
is not belief and young anything. I am on the verge of discov-
ery.

I want to paint this up   young   everybody done it.
It's an image   work at it like in a greenhouse or a boathut
                                    could read it.
I want to tell   heard a lot   so boring.
I could assemble   the joins so illegible.
Gulf didn't exist   no holocaust   diaspora a conspiracy.
You want you just plot with the like minded.

        Dear Ed
        I like what I know
        half tired and so beautiful a bored pogo.
        Change happens so fast I don't bother.
        Thought of everything
        everything thought up. No heroes.
        Directories are free. Why bother.

Young thinking young   anything could
be life   and little and little life
little easy I love my life.

Distribution of Credit Hours:

Core Math-sci	171
Military Science	7
Hum Crses	20
Youth	491

My quick answer to most young people as to why we have live boxing is that we are training young fighters. That's our life and our purpose, to train a young man to be a living leader on the field of combat. It's a very dangerous thing. And you young out there don't learn to live or to fight out of a book. There's only one way and that's to burn 'em. When you give a young guy a punch on the nose, this is basic communication. Bells. Hear 'em. I tell the plebs this kind of thing when I talk to them. When you are young enough and spunky enough you can punch people on the nose. Wham. There is no question in the other guy's mind what the hell you are trying to tell him. He understands what your purpose is. You learn. He learns. Don't quit, keep going! This is defence. This is stamina. This is the purpose of live boxing. Get this stuff underneath what you know as fast as you can. You've got to look after the future. It's your future. It's wonderful. Don't say a word now. Hit them. Just hit them.

Young no device to get anywhere
no rebellion no target
no overthrowing bar war
no change that great icon laid
no searching everything ready
why invent it's invented
no boundaries all soft and
melted   Picasso
moved perspective so frequently history
gave up   Picasso is in a book.
Culture like a supermarket
Pound among the potatoes   new made it new
new it's new enough.

Huge paintings, Rimbaud, 70% of the world with an erection.

Who cares in fog, don't see it.
life and little life your life
believe me
being young could be
anything.

from THE CHENG MAN CH'ING VARIATIONS

Cheng Man Ch'ing coming home down the alleyways. Walking. One foot in front of the other. All the weight swinging across his legs like water. Left thigh right thigh no sound. You'd expect bubbles. But nothing. One foot in front of the other. Cheng Man Ch'ing putting his foot down like he wasn't putting it anywhere other than where it was. Down. Positive. Intended. Positive intention. Head clear. Stillness after rain. All the aches and age settled. For now. Following the breath in and then out. Silence like darkness. Darkness like silence. Head up. Top of the spine. Walking home.

Cheng Man Ch'ing is a big man. For his race. But no one would mention that in liberal Britain in a back lane and Man Ching walking home feet shoulder width apart getting them down onto the grit and ruined tarmac without making a sound. Someone had asked him once what would you do if you moved forward in the form and put your foot down on a twig or a stone. How would you go on? He had thought for a minute and said, softly, move the foot a bit. Simple. There was a grimacing. The answer had not gone down well. The moves were fixed, the form western immutable. But Cheng Man Ch'ing was Cheng Man Ch'ing, his own Cheng Man Ch'ing man.

In the dark Cheng Man Ch'ing looks like a burglar. Soft footed so smooth. Silent. But there is nothing in his arms, in his hands. They arrested him once for suspicion, Chinaman in back-lane, full of air and strength and slow slow might. Went nowhere. Cheng Man Ch'ing smiling like Buddha, full of patience and spirit and light. He was no spectral being nothing vague he was real. You could touch if he'd give up yielding like the wind like thick water. He never did. Palpable peace. Next moment. This moment. Last moment. Touch it. No room for doubt.

In his back pocket he kept a Yang family tree. Huge thing like a heating duct plan for an office block. Given to him by a Californian or an Australian. Forgot which. If you read it back he seemed to be descended directly from the First Patriarch. With paper you could prove whatever you wanted.

Cheng Man Ch'ing a measurable risk
Colours fast
No Preservatives
Operable at Altitudes
Subject to variations within batch
    but batch itself secure.
Sample in catalogue merely a guide
    using available printer's inks.
EU patent possible.
Do not use abrasives.
Protected under international convention.
Replica buried in sand under
Salt Lake City by way of insurance.

They got him back to the station and put him in the interview room with the Formica table and asked him about the thefts saying they'd seen him on the 9th floor using his Chinese sleight of hand to open triple-barred doors things had gone white in his eyes. He'd come to standing on the table like a golden cockerel or a tiger something the room empty. All fled. The charge was assaulting the police. He used the unbendable arm to get out.

Man Ch'ing could take his liver out. Self-surgery. Hands in among the sinews knowing just where to go. He wrote it up as an article for *Combat* magazine but they didn't pay him and the following month there were a whole float of letters published from doubters who suggested that he was a fraud yellow faker. Why didn't he take on an 8th Dan karate, bandages round his fist like first aid. He could not bother be bothered he was bothered. Cheng Man Ch'ing iron in the silk and him up off the floor vanished. Into the wall plaster. Gone.

Cheng Man Ch'ing Yang Master Spirited Away.
Chinaman Reduces Molecules To The Consistency of Damp Mist.
Tai Chi Teacher Uses Conjuring Trick At Contest.
Eastern Mystic Hypnotizes Audience.
Mass Hysteria Sweeps Country.
Unexplained Disappearance Baffles Doctors.
Boffins Beaten By Oriental In Balloon Trousers.

Man Ch'ing trying to laugh with a mouth full of mortar.

*

art

What brightens their eyes?
fame, money, applause.
Cheng Man Ch'ing is not interested in these
his eyes do not attach
why should   ny
                f
                    is stuff
          ch   p
                p
    art   is   t   art
        is   t
isn   n   art
                               t

he is concerned with concerning this
concerning. he is all breath
sometimes a rush of air
what does he need to   he needs to
doing   no   not doing
becoming.   he is the diamond sutra
without thinking.   motes from his skin

95

Cheng Man Ch'ing flaking
through time   his eyes out of focus gleaming
he is at the one point

we are out here in our
bones chairs   knots of sinew

we are full of art
he is empty

*

Big crowd. Cheng Man Ch'ing in his huge Chinese trousers room for four legs and multiple genitalia. Available nowhere made by his old mother in Hopei Province. The black leaching out slowly as the material thinned. Dye in water. Smoke. His legs full of cat's strength but big. All the class looking expectantly as Cheng Man Ch'ing explains that all this and this is not really anything. If you travel far enough it stops having substance becomes nothing becomes something. This. Simple. You'll learn. They all nod. He nods. They smile. This. He lifts up his arm. There is hush. This this is an arm, this is, he says. This.

FROM FIVE HUNDRED COBBINGS

O captain! My Cobbing! Our folding scam is done
My Cobbolo singing

Cobbing: a term used to describe experiments in fun first developed in the 1950s which work primarily through the randomness of the poem. 'Cobbing begins by being aware of ambient pleasure as a structural agent.' 'Cobbing folds.' 'Cobbing oscillates.' 'Call this art can you read this.' 'Cobbing do it does it in writing and he sings.'

Cobbing is the strength
Cobbing between calm and catastrophe
Cobbing still presumed
Cobbing obtains incredible variety
Cobbing is a surprise
Cobbing a visiting psychiatrist
Cobbing difficult to reconcile
Cobbing does not form a selfish concept
Cobbing is a strange attractor
Cobbing always bothers
Cobbing in ceaseless motion
Cobbing with light poise
Cobbing exists
Cobbing a string
Cobbing so many difficulties
Cobbing a network of special fibre
Cobbing originates on a wintry afternoon
Cobbing a nonelephant animal
Cobbing's paradigm shift
Cobbing's red spot roaring
Cobbing under normal conditions
Cobbing it's a simple example
Oh my little Cobbing
my lovely Cobbing
my soft sweet Cobbono
my curling Cobbono
my curling Cobbing

Cobbing with bows and hearts
my great hearted Cobanovitch
Cobbing the stone throat
blue-eyed great coated
honeysuckly Cobbono
sugar sweet man Cobonsing
Cobbonot with eyes like diamonds
saucers
honey babe
that thing
Cobbing scented
Cobbing perfumed
great arm-pitted Cobbing
Cobbing caves
liana creeping Cobinsing
hoary Cobbing roaring
roaring roaring
Cobbing he roaring man

rows with Cob
    not
    no Cob
    that's terrible
    Cob you can't
    shut the Cob up
    Cob Cob Cob Cob off
    off Cobbing
    off running

How Cobbing manipulates: by tearing, by scorching,
by applying himself in drips, by partially being pasted,
by drinking, by splattering, by floating on water,
by being crumpled and crushed, by coming upon himself
suddenly, by being rubbed against a textured surface,
by smoking, by being found torn and battered or
jerked up at random from a great worthless stack, by
leaking, by draining, by being punctured and oozing,
by gushing in staccato leaps, by bounding, by being

incised, by roaring in plastic liquid, by emulsifying
boldly among tattooed supporters, by openly glinting,
by masking, by gilding, by frottage, fumage, froissage
and flottage, by fragmenting randomly, by scarifying,
by howling, by sifting, by cobbling, by groping, by
wobbling, by burnishing, by cushioning, by castellating
by mordant gilding, by counterstretching, by popping,
by proofing and adding, by chipping, by coating, by grinding,
by rendering with tar wash, by bathing in spirits, by
mildly mouldering, by setting fire to trousers, by
sanding, by fusing, by bubbling up smudged, by enumerating,
by translating, by jumping, by swimming, by eating and
by spitting and by coughing a lot and printing.

Cobbing Obstinate Brilliant Brutish Instant Negative Guru
Obstinate Cobbo Negative Brilliance
Brilliant Instant Cobinate Neverblume
Brutish Guru Brilliant Carbonium
Instant Obstinate Obcob Negation
Negative Collegiate Brutish Gurilization
Guru Cobinate Instant Obstinance

Cobnot	Brilliant	Instart	Brussel
Oblong	Cobon	Nightly	Brightness
Brilliant	Incy	Cobnob	Neurologist
Bristling	Gulper	British	Cadmium
Insisting	Obstinancy	Obcob	Neggelly
Negonot	Calling	Bristle	Gulpers
Glue	Carbon	Instant	Obolly

Cobolblot
Coboning

Cob'n	Oblate	Ill-timed	Nostril
Oblog	Cod	Nilly	Blimps
Brill	Ing	Cup	Nonprinter

Broshy	Gull	Brit	Cruncher
Inside	Old	Obcob	Naff
Not	Crip	Brot	Glick
Glom	Cog	It	Ob

No scientific Cobbing can ever be conclusively
refuted, since one can always adjust other
Cobbings to protect it.

Cob	Obb	Brat	Brut	It	Knee	Glass
Cob	Obb	Bring	Brong	Ins	Nog	Glam
Cob	Obb	Bing	Brang	In	Nog	Ung
Cob	Obb	Bin	Bong	In	Nig	Ang
Cob	Obb	Bin	Bang	In	Nin	Ning

Cobbing	Ordinary	Beastful	Bombastic	Intimidating	Nestling	Gnome
Cobolo	Ossified	Biaxia	Blinkered	Ineffable	Neighbour	Gnu
Codrobin	Occupied	Benedictine	Benevolent	Internal	Nomadic	Gimlet
Cobang	Onamato	British	Blighted	Infectious	Nonconc	Gip
Cobwhistle	Odled	Bingwung	Banging	Injured	Noggined	Giraffe
Cobbing	Oldfash	Beatup	Buttered	Infamo	Nightly	Grimalki

Conglomerate Cobbing Gangleader No Parts
Cobbing on his zoot horn mr rollo pushing
Cobbing solo

How does he think this Cobbing
one Cobbing follows another
Cobbing knows ether doesn't exist
Cobbing interrelated pessimistically.
Who will Cobbing meet, how will he do his laundry,
    what will he eat this Cobbing will he
    exhibit syllogisms fax Socrates his
    button pattern engage in the inspired abstract

Cobbing against the future neither bedroom slippers
nor parallels Cob the moment
yang Cobbing pouring it out.

Mambo Cobbing body wiggle
Begin the Cobano rumbolo
not all Cubans are Cobbings

Milonga Mobolo Tango Cobontra
Los Trios Indios Cobongos
Cobbing one step
Cobbing one step
Cobbing stood quick Cobbing

Cob for private pleasure
Cob for rebellion
Cob lust competitive dancing

he seems bolder old Cob
august body international sportsman
runner shifter prancer.

Sound poet Cobbono dances

I lurve my lurve my little Cobo
lurve my lurve my lurvely
my lurvely dancing Cobbono

Cobomox
–   proprietary broad-spectrum treats rips and spoons

Cobotrane
– antiseptic preparation fragrance dimithicone addled with tone
  broad hand smudges enlargements salt-sacks floating arm chairs

Coboticosteroid
– Synthetic secretion from kringle euphony chrispolo chrysantheum
myriad cohensive confluences

Cobisterine
- capsule convulsions mile tunnel roar specific. Dizziness followed
by wild bouts. Demonic trolley.

How does Cobbing keep going in the face of advesity?

Fun.

How does Cobbing stay strong?

Copies his arm flexes the muscles uses the enlarger moves the fingers
as the Cannon scans colour selects fudges. Runs hundreds. His arms
are famous.

How does Cobbing cope with fame?

Woke up and was still famous. Fast, fest. Has never slowed. Gives
autographs in bars, on trains and planes.Once, full of whisky, in a high-
rise somewhere south of the river was mistaken for Chairman of the
Council of Ministers Uzbekistan, N.M. Khudayberdyev, and unwilling
to forgo the honour spoke Cobbono imitation Uzbek-Russian for five
minutes, gave a stream of autographs to eager locals bearing copies of
The Sun, beermats and used brown envelopes. Fame and not-fame. A
great swirling. Zen master of the one pointed Cobbono. No car.
Walks. Uses the bus.

How does Cobbing remember what he says?

The goosebumps line up. The threads waft don't they? His computer
never helps. His old technology. He tries hard sometimes you can see
it on the wall by the phone. He thinks it over like a great drum
turning, bending bits and out of space time. He was never much inter-
ested in this maybe he should. When he goes out he forgets.

How does Cobbing travel?

Bootstraps no buckles. Read the book if you don't read the book you will never know.

Could he translate himself?

The Cobbing Le Cobbing.

How does Cobbing dry out?

The strong winds in off the Azores make a funnel effect. This multiplies under low pressure, moving large masses of air downwards in geo-spirals known as blotting. Cobbono is a great practitioner. The five-hundred miles per hour wind. The five-hundred foot rain storm. The five-hundred volt lightening. The five-hundred degree Cobbing.

How does Cobbing drive?

When young he loved cars. The oil smears on the mechanics' hands. The way the vehicles leaked, wouldn't start, smoked, made people stop and jump in the street. He liked in particular the sounds from the exhausts, the rattle of the pistons, the scratching cams and the fluted wave the air made as it crashed around the bonnet's vents. For a time he considered car building as a career, looked up engineering at the library, visited the Morris works. He wandered the dreaming spires with a head full of body panels and the smell of gasoline in his nose. He took easily to overalls with their embroidered badges, the big band hairstyles, the fingers black like Bridget Riley prints. What blew it were the manuals. Hu geform al texs fullo fendfloats. fe elerga uges, id ling, tor sionbars and torques. Cobbing coul dntre sisttea ringthe maparta ttheseams. Hisid eaof work would be to cut up and reassemble, to realign, the push the written direction to its limits, and then some. Edges were edges were edges were what were edges they were edges were were were edges and then again edges were they they certainly were edges were what he edged he edged and edges were was were will won't will will will will were edges always edges little edges these edges these wonderful edges of what were will were edges always edges they were edges he was what they were what these edges edges edges were what he he he edges were what he admired admired edges were what edges edges edges edges edges edges edges edges edges were what he admired. In an industry based on assembly lines and constant testing such attitudes were frowned on. Poor Bob. Hold them and the door would be shown. Cobbing head of rubber bellows, snap rings, clamp bolts, clutch flywheels and splendid beautiful gaskets like the crack of bolts, the crow of birds, the chants of indians turned his face towards a different career.

How does Cobbing cut?

A term used to describe experiments in fun first developed in the 1950s which work by tearing and by scorching. Cobbing begins by floating on water. Pushes then punctures the randomness of the piece. Cobbing invents clouds is a strange attractor always bothers. Cobbing in ceaseless motion safe in the sea. Coming upon himself after some time. Not tattooed but spliced.Cobbing oscillating. Hearing how it sounds. Safe unsafe it's the one.

How does Cobbing avoid headaches?

Cobbing puffs his cheeks out.
Cobbing frowns.
Cobbing glares.
Cobbing bites his nails.
Cobbing screws his eyes up.
Cobbing scowls.
Cobbing grates his teeth.
Cobbing collates (this is not the same as publishing).
Cobbing sneers.
Cobbing weeps (this is not the same as crying).
Cobbing pokes.

Cobbing has intercourse (this is not the same as loving).
Cobbing sniffs.
Cobbing nods his head a lot.
Cobbing lusts (this is not the same as desiring).
Cobbing converts.
Cobbing staples (this is not the same as eating).
Cobbing possesses.
Cobbing rushes around (this is not the same as running around).
Cobbing plays games like chess.
Cobbing is sarcastic.
Cobbing distributes (this is not the same as performs).
Cobbing silently disapproves.
Cobbing stays in The Engineer.

Who are the great influences on Cobbing's creative career?

George Herbert, Dick Higgins, Stefan Themerson, Nick Zurbrugg, Mike Gibbs, Dom Sylvester Houédard, Paula Claire, Eric Mottram, Peter Mayer, T.E. Hulme, Plato, Paul de Vree, Max bense, R. Jakobson, Eric White, Shorter Oxford Dictionary, Ernest Fenollosa, Ezra Pound, Hans Arp, Victor Shklovsky, Marcel Jousse, Naum Gabo, Max Bill, Jan Tschichold, Le Corbusier, André Hodier, Antoine Golea, Oyvind Fahlström, Eugen Gomringer, Emmett Williams, Jonathan Williams, Raoul Hausmann, Balzac, Glyn Pursglove, Maurice Denis, Kurt Schwitters, Viktor Vladimirovich Khlebnikov, Hugo Ball, Stephen Bann, Ardengo Soffici, Carlo Belloli, Augusto de Campos, Decio Pignatari, Haroldo de Campos, John Barth, E.E.Cummings, Ernst Jandl, Edwin Morgan, Charles Olson, Ian Hamilton Finlay, Anslem Hollo, Jerome Rothenberg, Reinhard Döhl, Franz Mon, Edward Lucie-Smith, Neil Mills, George Steiner, Ludwig Wittgenstein, Aldous Huxley, Ana Hatherley, Lee Harwood, Porfirius Optatianus, Trista Tzara, François Rabelais, Lewis Carroll, Henri Chopin, Christian Morgenstern, Man Ray, Stéphane Mallarmé, Kingsley Amis, Helmut Heissenbuttel, Seiichi Niikuni, Josef Honys, Filippo Tommaso Marinetti, H.N.Werkman, Alan Riddell, John Sharkey, Bernard Manning, Jiri Valoch, Claus Bremer, Paul Sheerbart, William S. Burroughs, Brion Gysin, Jeff Nuttall, Tom Phillips, Lily

Greenham, Dr Richard Beeching, Pierre Garnier, Bill Griffiths, Luigi Russolo, Bernard Heidsieck, François Dufrêne, Ted Hughes, Michael McClure, Jean-Louis Brau, Isidore Isou, Ronaldo Azeredo, Luiz Angelo Pinto, Mathias Goeritz, Pedro Xisto, Hansjorg Mayer, Aram Saroyan, Ladislav Novak, Julian Blaine, The Five Satins, bpNichol, Robert Lax, Paul de Vree, Miriljub Todorovic, Stuart Mills, Reinhard Döhl, Andrei Voznesensky, John Furnival, Saunders Lewis, The Four Horsemen, Karl Trinkewitz, Jean-Claud Moineau, Kenelm Cox, Gertrude Stein, Archduke Rainier, St. Augustine, Abbot Abbo of Fleury, Guillaume Apollinaire, Lajos Kassak, Marcel Duchamp, Alfred Bester, Ernest Marples, Asger Jorn, Alan Brownjohn, George Macbeth, Jeremy Adler, Michael Seuphor, Jack Kerouac, Äke Hodell, Bengt Emil Johnson, Jackson Mac Low, Mary Ellen Solt, Seigfried J. Schmidt, Iolo Morganwg, Bill Bissett, Rupert Loydell, The Eric Dolphy Big Band, Guy Schraenen, Anton Artaud, Ludwig Harig, Peter Fnich, Gregory Corse, Jin Cage, Rupert Crawley, Ribbin Fludd, Allow Ginsing, Victory Whogo, Robo Modlesgillingani, Holy Nagy, Jam Jin Jars, Willhelm Worsworth, Losing Zukfrostski, Arrigo Lora Totino Tabulated, Muddy Waters, Chubby Checker, Crippled Hard-Armed Davies, Stan Rosenthal and Eric Clapton.

How does the poet organise his time?

Smell of apples. The white sheet. The sharpened stick. The tape loop. The ready screen. Bookcase, cheese plant, vase, carpet, wall, space. He uses this for walks in the park, for conversations about dogs and repairs and pensions. Pulls the phone de-wires the bell lies to friends. Big blue window and the trees and the sky. Time in the great chair waiting to pounce. Scratched up Turner bugger the way distress. Sinking away in a stroboscopic shower. Hours like earrings, like roses, like pollen blowing. Time stretching. The copier toner bottle lasts a thousand years.

How does Cobbing cut?

A term used to describe experiments in fun first developed in the

1950s which work by splattering and being crumpled. Cobbing begins by floating on water. Cobbing manipulates the edges of the poem. Cobbing invents clouds is a strange attractor always bothers. Cobbing in ceaseless motion. Safe in the draining sea waving not reading but shouting not singing but thinking. Coming upon himself after some time. Not tattooed but spliced not stuck but unravelling. Cobbing oscillating. Hearing how it sounds. Absolutely unsafe. It's the one.

Cobbing's Closed System:

Repairing the lawn mower
Organising a file system
Planning a membership campaign
Fixing the copier
Drinking
Filling the paraffin heater
Arriving
Coat buttons
Cats

Cobbing's Open System:

Making jokes
Exploding
Not knowing the rules
Flowers
Head
The lecture on buddhism
Turning
Henri Chopin
food

Cobbing's band:

cob (tpt)
cobn (flhn)
cob (bell)
obob (p solo)
ing (toth)
cobm (bugle)
cobn (tb; clo; cbsspn)
cobn (acc. jig, footo)
cobn (bj, tongue vib)
cobn (wbd)
cobn (phcbr jam)
cobn (nse)
cobn (spt)
cobn (Cypriot bread)
cobn (wallpaper)

Ahmed Abcobbo and the Solomonic quintet
Roland Cobanovitch
Zoot Horn Cobdunski
Big Lips Bing Boppo
Cripled Hard Armed Cobbono
Hannibal Cobarnish Petersen
Cannon Cannon (mgr)

ggs chp (wknds) enqr wthn

Does he win?

Cobbing begins in fun. In ceaseless motion. A term used to describe experiments first developed in the 1950s. Cobbing invents. Not tattooed but spliced not stuck but sprayed and shifted not unmannered not rich but unravelling. Cobbing is the strength between calm and catastrophe. Safe not waving. Hearing how it sounds. Safe in the draining sea waving not reading but shouting not singing. Moving not stopping. Does he win he doesn't he cuts he marks. Some people

spend all their lives being tired. Cobbing folds his splices cuts copies.
He has time in a toner bottle. He invented the cut-up. He has told the
Americans. He has stains. He has discovered a new universe inside
our old one full of rich Cobbono. In ceaseless motion. Fun. Folding
scams. Experiments in random Cobbolo. Cobbing winning.

So where is he?

Cobbing the mark maker staining
translucent Cobbing shifting saturated Cobbing
Cobbing intense harmonious maker marker
complementary, harmonic and discordant contraster
Cobbing biased, tinted, the square cut
the margins sliding, the stained cut,
Cobbing shifting marks, staining Cobbing
straining cuts, square marking, stained Cobbing
cut harmoniously, slid, rubbed
Cobbing cut shift cut shift
splice reverse touch trip
make mask slice rip cut shift
cut shift cut shift cut shift
cut shift cut shift cut shift

Cobbing cuts

Cobbing slips

five hundred Cobbings

cut

shift

slip

mix

LUNCH TIME

Subjects assume time passes at different speeds. 'It's slow this morning.' 'It drags terrible, this time to one o'clock.' 'When it gets like this the day is never going to end.' 'It'll be hours until we get a break' (actually only twenty minutes). Time is flexible. Lunch is always assumed to run at more than one velocity. The thirty minutes preceding one o'clock (the time lunch break commences) can take two hours. In the food queue ten minutes takes twenty; at a table the time actually consuming food stretches out as long as food remains before the subject. Once the plate is empty time contracts again.

'It's five past eleven', 'That clock's gone slow again. It's nearly ten past. Jack, don't you make it nearly ten past?' 'That's not slow. That's right.' 'What, is it only five past?' 'That's right.' 'Oh! Only five past.' The official time for dinner is one o'clock, and the official time for getting ready for it is five minutes to; actual preparations start a long while before that. The mass of the sun curves space-time in such a way that although earth follows a straight path in four-dimensional space-time, it appears to us to move along a circular orbit in three-dimensional space. Between half-past twelve and five to one the cloakrooms are locked. The idea of this is to prevent people getting ready before the appointed time.

What actually happens is this. Each event is labelled by a number called 'time' in a unique way, and all good clocks agree on the time interval between two events. However, the discovery that the speed of light appears the same to every observer, no matter how they were moving, or where they were, cloakroom or machine shop, leads to the abandonment of absolute time. Each observer has their own measure of time recorded by a clock they carry. Clocks carried by different observers do not necessarily agree. Time is a personal concept. What actually happens is people go to the cloakrooms before they are locked. They do not distinguish between the forward and backward directions of time. What happens is they return to the bench and do nothing whatever for half an hour, so as not to get their hands dirty again. The last thing they need is to wash again before lunch.

PROBLEMS OF GRAVITY

Theorists believe (bowdlerise) that the (only)
solution (softening) (lime dissolution) may lie (may
sink) (may leave) not (never) in (under) quantizing
(manipulating) (sheering) (de-cladding) gravity
on its own (other) but in (on) developing
(re-cladding) (aluminium siding) (shingle-fixing)
a (the) quantum (literary) (political) theory
(structure) (dream) (ground bait) that (this)
incorporates (is) gravity (grease) and electromagnetism
(depression) together (apart) (apiece) (along)
(antipathy) with (without) other (all) (any)
fundamental (free) (phoney) forces (fuses).
Theorists bowdlerise (excavate) the (this) only
(only) (only) softening (unbolting) (splicing)
may sink (structure) (solidify) (steam off)
never (not) under (over) manipulating (moulting)
(wrist locking) gravity (chi) on its other
(only) but on (in) (on) (in) (under) (in) (over)
(in) (and) (in) re-cladding (gate-force)
(trouser-bend) (switch) a literary (feeble)
(frozen) dream (drown) this (those) is (is not)
grease (cow-gum) (tension) (tack) (easy-stik)
and (without) desperation (depression) apart
(along) (aspirin) without any (all) free (flight)
(foam) (folded) (fickle) (folded) (fractionated)
fuses (folded) forces (forces) forces (force).

ANTIBODIES

Action of antibodies against snake venom is simple: the antibody alone disarms the toxin. Antibodies can also neutralise bacteria. Zigzag structure ('The tape-recorder's treatment of the voice teaches the human new tricks of rhythm and tone' - Cobbing: *We Aspire To Bird Song*). Antibodies can combat some viruses by binding to them and preventing them from invading cells. These bindings of idea on idea have immense application. With the majority of micro-organisms, the antibody needs help to kill the invader. Examples include the George Harrison 'My Sweet Lord' settlement, Glyn Jones's unresolved gull's wing action against Hugh MacDiarmid, pale revision John Cooper Clarke's 'Subterranean Homesick Blues'.

Further successes cause inflammation and bring other immune cells into the infected area. There is a possibility of using cells to carry out the binding activity deliberately. Immune systems are taught to 'listen' to artificial activity and remember the pattern using cell displacement. This process is known as 'thymic education' where the immune system, now unable to attack its own cells, can readily recall the intellectual associations of previous chance activity in others and replicate them. This is undoubtedly an emotional driven creative activity. Some immunologists believe that any chance derived output remaining and bound to the body's own molecular system is either further converted or destroyed. Others disagree and believe the educative process lies elsewhere. Their reporting of these matters can be virulent and disturbing. For many participants this is simply the point. Exactly what happens during their thymic education remains gloriously uncertain.

AUTOMATISM

So much of our lifetime is spent
exploiting automatism. Instinct,
habit and improvisation enable us
to perform without the need for
deliberation. No activity
in this field without certificate.
But the deep-rooted mechanistic antipathy
to the idea of an active, useful
subliminal self leads the symptoms of
sensory and motor automatism to
be treated as pathological. The splatter
regarded as heresy. How can.
Mummy I saw Jesus. The sprawl of light.
Huge. I see what I remembered.
The hysterical fugue trench
failure incurable except by
discharge. The fugue modernism
breath of wind. Total collapse not a
characteristic of giving in. Fugue of
standardising, unifying, rationalising,
simplifying, universalising replaced
by pluralism and complexity. I do
not use consciousness to direct.
No love of fieldwork. There is a
need to discover a meaning for
life which is not primarily connected
with interpersonal relationships.
Freeze into fraudulent. Fugue of light.
The piece ends.

BALLOON

Scientists sent up balloons that got lost; the instruments sometimes measured the temperature of the balloons themselves rather than the sky. The interests of the scientists would often diverge from that of their projects. Sometimes these scientists would exhibit disturbing traits. Frequently they would be paranoid, over suspicious, chronicler-vigilant; show extreme mood swings; have periods of extreme anxiety or report quasi-hallucinations while on the verge of their discoveries. These scientists would be particularly concerned with developing their own points of view autonomously, protective of their inner worlds against premature scrutiny and criticism by others. Their problem is, of course, the self. Can the self remember the direction it runs for the whole of a life time? Can the self be more than the random jittering of electrons inside any material? The self is probably the most bizarre thing in nature. It can defy gravity, run up slopes, pass back through time, replicate itself endlessly in a blinding blizzard, invent a million tortuous justifications, dance for days on the head of a pin. Smudges, smears, fractures, deviation, dark shift, dark shrapnel, dark side. It's got all of these. The balloon came down in the trees at the end of the field. Said inside IN THE INTERESTS OF SCIENCE RETURN TO PO BOX 194 LIVERPOOL. Didn't do that. Did this.

THE PROBLEM OF SUCCESS

Fashions play such an essential role in the sociology and in the funding of our successes. A specialised subject (such as linking hands around the Pentagon, rolling marbles under police mounted horses or bringing down surveillance helicopters with kites flown on heavy gauge sea fishing line) comes into fashion for a few years, and is then dumped. In the meantime the field has been invaded by swarms of people who are attracted by the possibilities of fame rather than the ideas involved. Early examples of innovation (Peter Mayer's Yin-Yang Cube printed on impossible to assemble newsprint; ingested banana skins as hallucinogenic; wasp musical instrument formed by trapping the insect in a jar covered with an amplifying membrane) are superseded by pre-formed plastic, shrink-wrapped, aided, over simplified, black and white versions and other sophistications. The intellectual atmosphere changes. I shall give you one personal example of this. After the publication of my note on fishing line political determination referred to above a colleague told me 'It is quite a successful paper – I tried to look it up in the University library, and it had been cut out of the journal with a razor blade.'

ACKNOWLEDGING SOME OF THE SOURCES

The way light-cone tipping leads to time travel is shown in *figure 7.6* (see Fisher, Allen[b. 1944] *Future Exiles*). In this versions of a chance diagram, two space dimensions are indicated, with the flow of time, as usual, going up the page. Only the future halves of the light cones are shown, to keep the picture simple. The time axis also represents the world line of a massive, rapidly rotating naked singularity. Fisher makes one form from a rolled and glued copy of *The Financial Times,* an activity quite appropriate to his methods. This paper tube has an effect in a universe of fragments bound together by greed, hatred, desire and worldliness. There is no evidence discernible, mathematical or otherwise, of any specific belief system. Rather, the whole process replies on chance operators. Randomness becomes order.

Far away from the singularity, where gravitational field is weak, the light cones open out into the future in the way it is for flat space-time. But the closer you get to the spinning singularity, the more the cones bend and tip to the centre. This is much in the style of fugitive publishing. Fisher, following his own activities in this field, reports many common phenomena to be unstable. I recall him removing his trousers mid-performance to reveal a second identical pair beneath. A displacement activity totally ignored, although certainly registered, by his audience.

For an observer far away in flat spacetime, watching events in this region of the distorted centre, the roles of composition and appreciation in such a strong field can be seen to interchange. Composition begins to bind itself to both the perceiver and the perceived before bending itself out of all conventional recognition. Fisher indicates arm movements by special symbols printed in the margins. His determinism is undetermined. 'There is nothing I can do about it,' he says, 'There is nothing *to* do'.

From USEFUL (1997)

TALK ABOUT NICE THINGS

She has to be helped from the car now
muscles like knitted scarves
her knees spread, wind wisps in her hair.
Her voice slips as vocabulary turns
to slush. She told me books
were too big. She liked talk
about nice things   nothing   how it was.
Her day shuffles dust, rearranges
antimacassars, grand rubber gloves.
When night falls television is
memory flickering on her walls.
She butters bread. The word for
love won't come, too distant. Sleep
stands like a dolmen in the hall.

SUMMER SCHOOL

In the writer's class
the world has retired.
None of the students
fit the chairs.
Age has intervened.
    A woman with a chest
    like a coal sack sings
    cracked extracts from
    Gilbert and Sullivan. I am
    too polite to stop her.
They all seem to have
been coming here for
decades and no one
ever improves.
    We attempt a haiku
    for brevity. A dragon
    in a floral dress reads
    hers as if she were hailing
    a taxi. She is a thespian.
    The back row have
    misunderstood and supply sonnets.
    The man with the limp and
    the stained trousers talks about
    the war against the
    nip in Singapore.
I read Sylvester's
    rendering of Bashō,
    Frog
    Pond
    Plop
ripple on ripple
a gulf away
from self-confession or
stuff about tramps.

It is a matter of echoes
I tell them.
A haiku suggests,
obliquely,
is full of waves.
A harridan in the front row
puts her hand up.
Yes? Am I getting through?
Load of crap, she says.

HEART

warps of the heart
the unfulfilled heart
the bent heart

Late at night looking west when the Shirelles
come on the radio   the fridge clicking   the down
pipe loose   moon   stars   like it has always been.

Sometimes the heart is so prominent that it
becomes a log wedged across the chest.

Does the heart have its own memory own
fears its own ghost way of talking
getting things done?

heart sways like a sabre
heart beats like a gong

In the morning rain running Lou Reed on
the Walkman chest a great house heart some
monster to be afraid of   I was in the weights
room sweat searing when my father died   my heart
engorged   his like a cold clam. How do you
breathe, he'd asked me   afraid in the night
for the first time in 70 years   sink the shoulders
relax let it come   this technique
the only thing in a life I'd ever really given
him and in the end even this hadn't worked.

Sitting in the car park in the rain his
hat in a Tesco bag   trembling   heart moving
away from me faster   like an accelerating train.

The traces have smiles on them
Smudges of voice   the imperfect
Touch   all that remains.

FISTS

When I form a fist
the index knuckle still sings
from the red mist a year ago when
I punched a hole in the wardrobe door.

We've exchanged hangers since. Mine are
radio aerial diamonds.

Out the back are the boxes I won't
look in. Half a menu; sea shells;
kid's first shoe.

Time is in the next room, hissing like
a cistern. My fist is another fist now, of
course, the body renewed totally every
few years. Different bones, different
skin.

I pass you your junk mail. You put it
in your bin.

I walk behind people in crowds, imitating
their steps, not being me, seeing what it
is to be them.

It works, occasionally, now and then. You
don't recognise me by the veg
in the supermarket.

My fist in the frozen peas. You with him.

THE WRITER ON HOLIDAY WITH TWO TEENAGERS SENDS A POSTCARD HOME

Dear All,

You wouldn't like it here. Too much like the brochure, full of brightness and heat. Each day by eleven when the cloud has flaked westwards the sun is all we can see. We are at a cove, an artificially sanded rock inlet filled with the tideless Med. This totteringly Spanish precursor to EuroDisney has been overrun by German car workers and is now one of the nosiest places on earth. Demonic children, armed with giant crocodile beach rafts and submariner masks the size of televisions, roar in circles. Housefrau like blistered sea-lions howl vociferously while their lobster husbands pay, what must be to them and their brilliant economy, virtually nothing to rent rust-blotched sombrillas and frayed tumbonas. Balearic heaven.

In the short time I have been here I have seen off Updike's *Rabbit*, Styron's *Sophie* and Keneally's *Ark*. My children have crouched in the shade gamely chasing the Brothers Mario and manipulating stacks of Tetris blocks. I can discourse on the holocaust, on guilt and the love and the place of god in this burning mess. They can move their fingers with a dexterity I'll never match. Culture changes. We drink cola stuffed with ice and slivers of lemon. I doze. With the love that only close family can show they berate each other for being alive.

It has been a week of angst, blame, teenage dissidence and untrammelled rage. Me, burning in the swordfish-sun, attracting wasps of abuse like a melting sweet. You slap-headed queer shut up I'm telling you pay the bill you wanker don't make such a bloody fuss everyone looks why should bloody bugger bastard let me tosser you cock.

There are no clouds. Television is in Spanish. The bus to town is full.

Sometimes in small moments of respite arrived at by accident when the abuse softens into unwashed teenage sleep I reflect on how the great leaders of men must have skins like bunker concrete and ears as selective as Russian radio dials.

Sand in your suitcase, grit in your bedclothes, size nine green giant athletic footwear across your last fresh towel, suncream in your passport, your pen a blunt dart, your half-finished novel by Stan Barstow frisbeed out to sea at noon.

Virulence rises like steam as the Med winks ever bluer in the slashing heat. On the horizon a white yacht grazes. Despite my tan I feel soft and bloodless. The Germans are buying everyone huge Minorcan frankfurters and splashing them with luminous mustard brought from home. I buy a three-day old Sunday newspaper for £5.50 and find the magazine, the arts supplement and the books section have all been jettisoned to save air weight. I swear a bit myself.

In the distance I can hear the hotel entertainer on loud hailer encouraging the Aryans by the pool to polka faster. The week smokes on like a three funnelled cruiser. I camouflage myself with Bronzotan. The beach is at least uncompromisingly topless. I adjust my dark glasses and permit a smile. Fucking homosexual shouts my son.

Best
P.

THE STEPS

In front of the museum
free now for Cardiffians
where John Tripp hid
his bicycle clips among the pillars
and the statue of Lloyd George
greens slowly in the drizzle
I saw Tom Jones once
eluding fans among the bushes.
Heart of the Welsh universe
its white Portland replicated
perfectly in India
where the architect made a quick
rupee reselling his plans.
The past concentrates on these slabs.
Memory of marches, meetings, passions,
hired coaches like cream river-boats
the steps cut like a ghat on the Ganges.
When the sea rises
the tide will reach here with ease.

LAMBIES

The Wentloog Levels between Cardiff & Newport

Climb up, you can do it. Top of the sea wall
overgrown with foxtail, bent grass, cranesbill,
ribwort, speedwell. The fields here are flat, crossed
with reens foreign as Mars, taking the swamp away.
We walk single file. Shelduck on the
mudflats, groyne teeth, breakwater, boat-ribs,
wrecked hard-core, the slope to the sea estuary
toughened with skin of boulder rough as navigator's hands.

The ponds they've built for fish look real enough,
ditch and slack joined behind the Peterstone Sluice.
But up close their Disney geography belies the buckling
winds, neat angling piers made of log, clips
for catchnets, fences. The sea-board warning sign
rain eroded. Do Not. The path thickens with
heavy cock's-foot. As if we would.

The flats stretch away into sunlight alive with
thunder-cloud, waste mud like thrown paint. Cars
are smashed here, brick, city detritus, logs
drifted with scoured plastic, cans. Blue smoke off the
last beaches, gravel, waste concrete, sand.

Across the Channel the Somerset Levels as wrecked
as these. Distant hammering as some kid smashes
a bus shelter and the thug-roar of a high-cleated
Kawasaki carving across grass. Behind us chicaned,
traffic-calmed housing merges slowly with wilderness.
Gull overhead in a turning cloud. Soon they're gone.

ALL I NEED IS THREE PLUMS

apologies to William Carlos Williams

I have sold your jewellery collection,
which you kept in a box, forgive me.
I am sorry, but it came upon me
and the money was so inviting, so sweet
and so cold.

I have failed to increase my chest measurements
despite bar bells
and my t-shirt is not full of ripples.
I am sweet but that is no consolation.
Your hand is cold.

I did not get the job, your brother did.
He is a bastard I told him, forgive me.
The world is full of wankers, my sweet.

I have lost the dog, I am sorry.
He never liked me, I am hardly inviting.
I took him off the lead in the park and
the swine chased a cat I couldn't
be bothered to run after him.
Forgive me, I will fail less in the
future.

I have collected all the furniture I could find
and dismembered it in the grate, I am sorry
but I have these aberrations.
The weather is inclement. You have run out of
firelighters.
It's bloody cold.

Please forgive me, I have taken the money
you have been saving in the ceramic pig
and spent it on drink, so sweet and inviting.

This is just to say I am in the pub
where I have purchased the fat guy from
Merthyr's entire collection of scratch and win.
All I need now is three delicious plums.

Forgive me, sweetie,
these things just happen.

MEETING HER LOVER

I cannot talk to him about football
because I don't know enough. The game
roars on the television like a floundering
ship. I try books but he doesn't respond.
With his fat eyes he looks so dumb.
We try weather it's exciting as
tyre pressures and motorway routes.
Outside the sun is enormous.
His car is shit fast he tells me I
couldn't give a damn. On the
screen the goals mount like fever,
men embracing on the green sward.
You take her then, I say, as
if this woman is still something I
have a hold on. But he's not looking,
the game's being played again,
on and on.

TAKES GUTS

I thought all this would be okay
getting arseholed lunchbreak the going
back on the job and pretending I was
okay enough to work the sheet press.
You know the form: stand around pull
the lever piece of piss so long as you
don't fall in. As it was we'd put
Morgans' lunchbox through the
quarter-inch mill and stood it
like a Tom and Jerry thing in his
locker, bits of four-foot tomato
sandwich and pressed tin. Mickey had
filled the guy's bike frame with
industrial mercury. When he tried to
get it out of the rack he'd think his
arms had failed. The whole afternoon
was like this, paint fights and helium
gargling. A fucking hoot until I got
my coverall caught under the cutter
and since the travel-stop had unscrewed
lost a slice of gut. Through the pethidine
fog I can hear Morgans telling me
self-inflicteds don't count for benefit
and that I was too fat anyway. Wanker.
Wait till he gets to re-milling the failed
castings. His bucket has been wired direct
into the 240. No one's gone that far
before. Takes guts.

THE WAY IT GROWS

On mud and in shallow water
confined to gardens
in crevices on slopes
on waste ground and waste places
and waste woodland on hedgebanks
in shingle on sand in shaded limestone
and damp grassland near streams on
thin soils and salt marshes
on dry grasslands and bogs and coastal
cliffs in walls on the banks of ditches
on rubbish tips and sand dunes and
wet cliff ledges and rocky places
and thickets in woodland on riverbanks
and damp scrub and high ground and
shallow soils on grassy heaths and hill
slopes and marshy pools and salt marshes
and cornfields on flushes in low fore-dunes
and muddy creeks and estuaries and marshy
driftlines on dune slacks and muddy
edges in conifer plantation and beech-woods
and grasslands behind spoil-tips on marsh edges
and waste field banks and headlands
in brackish ditches and sown
roadsides on spray zones and
water reaches and acid tongues
on marshes under hedges on strew-floors
in distrusting argument and outmoded
pairings in damp boredom on child-trodden
guilt and urban crap dumps under piecemeal
thickets of antipathy, alcohol and despair in
marshy foreshores of misogynist sex and
tears and rage and endless duplicity
in the spray of other things and other strains
and other lusts and other needs.
When it doesn't feel right you throw it.
When it doesn't work you don't fix it you

dump it jesus when it ceases to flower
you mash it and in the mess of bog
and marsh inside you oh how it steams
oh how it leers.

STONE CLASPS

The leaf won't lift with the broom, frost laced, frozen to the quarry-tiled path. My father laid this out, told me how, appraised the door architrave, complained about the bare hall floor. I fixed it. He's gone.

This house is at the flux of three churches, one at each street end, another two roads off, length of a football field if you could stand high enough to shout. While my father lived, arriving in his gleaming cars, these stone clasps of god stayed invisible. Feast days they'd flush and shimmer, but their own fathers stayed deep inside them, full of the past.

I bend down and breathe warmth on the palmate lobes, unglue them with my own vital force. Three years since his voice echoed anywhere round here yet when I need to hear it, it's still there. I see the priests and pastors now walking to their sanctuaries. I recognise them by their steady gait, I know who they are. Their bodies are upright like antennae, they carry small packages in their arms. Their churches are half-empty but remain such strong places. I have gone to them and leant my hands to feel the spirit in their walls. Death can make you need. The chinks in your armour blink and at night, inexplicably, you fear.

The leaf comes free to leave a damp mark its own shape, a ghost. My father walks on between the churches. I see them waiting with their ancient faces. I look but that's all I do. I go in and replace the broom in the cupboard. It's much too soon.

THE RIVER

We travel. The new road runs high up over the estuary. You can watch the river touch the sea here. The blending of waters, not river, not sea; a rolling, two shaded place of suck and swirl. My companion talks of white-water rafting in Alaska and the excitement of free-falling 100 meters through churning rock, alone. But I'm only half listening. This river – Welsh, dirty, slow – ends like it began, like the Welsh do most things – not exactly, not precisely, in no single place, in no markable spot, no trigonometrical point, no reference, no marker, no writ, no underlined thrice signboard, but it does end. The river stops, amorphously, somewhere out there, in the blue grey mesh of the spinning world.

I hunted its source once amid the highest hills we have, hummocks, really, barely reaching 3000 feet, but wild enough. Up there, crossing ridge on ridge, expecting a bubbling I could put my fist to, I discovered instead a thousand sources, a great seeping, no one point I could mark with my boot heel. A meandering, a wonderful vagueness, like the sky, like the sea itself, like the void.

My companion tells me most countries have rivers bigger than this one. I tell her that doesn't matter at all.

PARTISAN

rydw i am fod blydi i am
rydyn ni rydw i rody i
rodney rodney i am
rhydyn am fod I am I am I am
rydw i yn Pantycelyn Rhydcymerau Pwllheli yes

I am bicupping mainly cym sticker ardvark
the dictionary cymro hirsuit weirdo
on fire arrested finger-pointed rhydych chi
imperialist long-nosed pinky cottagers

roeddwn i'n fine yn y bore oherwydd
y heddlu not able anyway little zippo
lager considerable influence
tried to burn it not enough alcoalcohol
corner shop four-pack Diamond White Red Stripe
brns your heart out

rudin wedi dysgu hen ddigon ol' mouldering
Welsh Saunders Mabinignog crap
nasty blydi books we're a digidol neishyn
smot superbod sam tan brilliant exampl

ac yn nawr?
bod ar y satellite no defense
carchar poms yn saesneg
dim yn gallu handlo'r cymraeg
rîl traditional blydi welshman

THE EXHIBITION

Man With Towel Drying His Tongue
oil on canvas 30" x 20"

Bright Nude With Crown
pastel on paper 10" x 16"

Self-Portrait With Star On Stick
mixed-media 40" x 60"

Triptych - Nudes Embracing, Nudes Struggling, Nudes Parting
oil on paper with felt roofing strips 30" x 8 yards

Self-Portrait With Stick and Ripped Shirt
pencil 2" x 2"

Portrait of the Artist As A Misogynist
tongue between teeth
oil on canvas with eyeliner applique and
glued beer cans
collection G. Broding

Views From Inside The Wardrobe
mixed media – tin bath, water and electric kettle element

This Is How It Is Now
instamatic assemblage of the artist looking miserable
in various parts of the city 40" x 30"
collection R. Knowles, private investigator

Untitled
body tattoo "I Love You" crossed out with blue biro
NFS

Small Man With Bottles
charcoal on burned paper 10" x 10"
collection the artist
print available, enquire at desk

Dark curtain for obscuring door.

RNLD TOMOS (*vcl, hca,* some *prse*) aka Curtis Langdon. 1913-2000. Gospel. Austerity tradition. Jnd Iago Prytherch Big Band (1959), gog, gap, bwlch, lleyn, tân, iaith, mynydd, mangle, adwy – mainly on Hart-Davis race label. Reissue Dent PoBkSoc Special Recommnd. Concert at Sherman support Sorley Maclean (*gtr, hrt clutching*) sold out. Fire Bomb tour Sain triple cd for D Walford Davies (*vcl, crtcl harmonium*) new century highspot. A pioneer of dark wounds and internal tensions. In old age bird song and reliable grouch. Stood, was counted, still no change. To live in Wales is to become un-assailable. 'An angel-fish' (Clarke). Expect retrospective, marvelling and statue.

SONNET NO 18

Eeeee e eeeeeee eeee ee e eeeeee's eee?
Eeee eee eeee eeeeee eee eeee eeeeeeooo:
Ooooo ooooo oo ooooo ooo ooooooo oooo oo Ooo,
Ooo oossss's sssss ssss sss sss sssss s ssss:
Ssssssss sst ttt ttt ttt tt tttttt tttttt,
Ttt ttttt tt ttt ttta aaaaaaaaaa aaaa'a:
Aaa aaaaa aaaa aaaa aaaa aaannnnn nnnnnnnn,
Nn nnnnnn, nn nnnnnn'n hhhhhhhhh hhhhhh hhhhhhh'h;
Hhh hh hrrrrrr rrrrrr rrrrr rrr rrrr,
Rrr rrri iiiiiiiii ii iiii iiii iill ll'll,
Lll lllll lllll llll lllm mmmmmm'mm mm mmm mmmmm,
Mmmd dd dddddd ddddd dd dddu uuuu uuuu'uu;
  Uu uuff ff fff fff ffggggg, gg gggg ggc ccc,
  Cc cccc ccyyy yyyy, www wwwv vvvvb bbbb pp ppkx.

WRITTEN OUT

There are five types of evil which come on
      us when we stop trying.
First is the formation of alliances
        to denigrate the wise works of others
        you recognise these.
Second is the way we luxuriate in new editions
        old songs like shiny beasts
        commas retreaded.
Third is an oppressive interest in charms, fate,
        it'll be alright on the night
        my puddings always rise God ordained it.
Fourth is judgement based on hearsay
        read nothing for twenty years
        nothing reported.
Fifth is lining up others
        into cabals of aged malfunction
        little more to say
        bar abrogation.
        There is nothing new under the sun
        and the sun is sinking.

It is all treacherous and immoral and
      you should distance yourself.

Until of course it becomes inevitable.

From FOOD (2001)

STATS

height down 10 mm
weight increase 2.1 kilo in 60 months
waist 32 to 34 maybe
pulse resting at 72 up 8
stretch reduction sit & reach 27 cm
vision 2.25/3.25
lung capacity 4.21 litres normal
grip strength 44 kgf
can sit w no movement 1 hr 30
flat mile averaged 7.1 seconds unhindered
erection angle 82° no windchill
40 x lifts in sets average
belief drop 15.5% alc. unit level 17 mean
1991 records show 32 29 41 82 (unattributed)
{compare 2015366 Finch (my father) 134 lbs in 1940
his only extant stat}
this data how I move from A to B
archaeology without suffering
the body elsewhere this is the dust

THE TAO OF DINING

We go into the restaurant and the bill is thirty
before we sit. The waiter sells us five pound
Chardonnay for thirty. The menu reads like a
language test. Understanding creeps we go
limp and warm. I want a full plate three bread
rolls I get a biscuit and a pool of yellow in its centre a
centimetred fish. We are dining because this is
intimacy and the alcohol helps. I want life
it's here. Snazz blues in the backdrop the
waiter skips. "You enjoy, monsieur?" He's
Australian. The bill is already sixty I don't care.
The wine is a symphony I have no way of
judging. Crème Brulée makes our hair shine.
Our fellow diners glow like angels,
our souls are singing.
The bill is somewhere I have never been before,
read with joy, signed with ecstasy,
the whole restaurant is smiling.
Someone said dining is all experience.
Lao Tzu that only the one you are in right now
has any importance. Outside it's raining.

WORDS BEGINNING WITH *A* FROM THE GOVERNMENT'S WELSH ASSEMBLY WHITE PAPER

a a assembly an assembly assembly assembly and assembly and assembly assembly assembly assembly assembly annexes and arrangements assembly and assembly affairs and authority accountability a achievement assembly autumn assembly a affect an an assembly assembly assembly and a alongside a an assembly assembly assembly allocate assembly and and acts assembly assembly assembly administrative agriculture a an annual and authorities and agency and authorities are accountable address assembly and answerable across assembly assembly assembly assembly assembly and arrangements are assembly assembly are assembly agriculture and and and and arts and annex a assembly approval assembly all after assembly assembly affairs and and assembly assembly and a and account appropriate assembly acts and are acts a assembly are assembly a authority and and able as and a assembly authorities agencies assembly able assembly assembly and a and and a a a assembly assembly and able able assembly about a assembly and a assembly as appointments also and assembly assembly as assembly assembly against as as able and authorities against and assembly are a and a assembly assembly and assembly assembly a affairs assembly authorities and and and and all and ahead and are across and as assembly and assembly a attuned a agency and authority authority and and and and and any agenda assembly a assembly able a a a adopting assembly and and are a authority and afford an ambitious and a an as as an and air and agencies assembly a and administration agency a and assembly agency already an all and and and agencies authority authority as a and and assembling and authority are agency acquired and and address an a a across and assembly and appoint agency a a assembly authorities at and agency and a and an agency assembly assembly agency arrangements and agency authorities a and attracting and and assembly action action action and a and a assembly assembly agenda assembly at all agenda assembly and and appointments also and are also a and a and an authorities agencies and advice advice approximate a assembly and at affairs annual a and assembly and actions assembly assembly assembly and a administering assessment advisory assembly and adequate appropriate appropriate areas and approximate arrangements are appropriate approximate appropriate arrangements and assembly art assembly are arrangements approximate appricimate appropin approximarly approximin approximit approximate appropinate appropriate approlution approximate apprealin approling approf appross apprit approx approximate appropriate arsembly approt approt apprit aparse amprim arsenit arsenit arsenit arsenit arsenit arsenit arsenit arsenit arsenit approximately assembly and arsen assembly all art and agriculture agenda appropriately alltittle all al aswoon apricot artle at assen ash arsenit assuitable assuage annual after amiddle approximate appealment apparliament arprat aprat art arse alltold approximate flatart anti anemia academic and averted arse art all assembly anti any attitudenal arseweakness all appropriate approximate approximate apripple affected arse affected all affected and any affected apathy apathy and responsibility for ancient monuments arses arses arses and wishing wells

THE STUDENT HOUSE

We arrive through thin snow to
my son's student house where
no one has been for three weeks.
The ice has turned the air to knives.
I find a ketchup-smeared plate
frozen at 45° in the unemptied
kitchen sink. A river of lager
cans flows down the hall.
As I stamp into the lounge
keeping my feet alive the ghosts
of dust come up around me like
children. The stains across the
sofa look like someone has died.
Amid the wrappers and old news
washing against the skirting I
spot the letter I sent up six-months
back. It's up to you, I wrote,
you are on your own now,
no one can do this for you,
something like that.
He enters the room in his ripped
jeans and shrunken sweat-shirt
fingers locked in his arm-pits.
Do we clear this place? Can't be bothered,
the energy has been
frozen out of us. He hands
me the torch. I go to the basement
to see if I can fix the boiler, no
longer in charge but still trying,
the fallen king. I light the pilot
and the heat comes back,
a kind of love, pressing us softly
as we stand saying goodbye
amid the junk mail in the hall.

SOUTH WALES HAIKU

Blowing graffiti
From the viaduct buttress
An autumn gale

Soccer fans gathering
Their talk has the richness
of cabbage soup

Old love on the hillside
His penis stuffed
With chrysanthemum

Month after month
On the councillor's face
A councillor's mask

Ice sky above B&Q
New fence post burn
In the breath of customers

Cherry blossom on the coal shed
Kid inside
Killing a cat

Outside the boarded church
Rolled carpet and piled chairs
The stack almost reaches heaven

His shaky arm
Lifts to the sky
Beer rusts the zip of his trousers

Sound of an old man
Cracking snails
Clear to the big dipper

Shadow of the pithead
A cricket, two greyhounds
And a thin man smoking

Man with a red face
On the 9.20
Dandelion in his button-hole

At the pond
Brazen frog and
Stone cat sniffing

Dim mynediad the farmer's sign
The cow parsley
Goes right on in

Two days of sun
Twat in his garden
With a hose

Man with a banner and a
Voice you cannot understand
Hands out tracts in the rain

In the heat an old woman
Queue jumps so slowly
No one speaks

Half a bike in the river
A frame chained to
A fence

No coal left
Out the back burning
The contents of his garden

The hands move so slowly
Is there more than this?
Unpacking frozen fish

Telling a joke
At the Lamb and Flag
Forgotten the ending

IRISH GUIDE TO WALES ERRATA

when you arrive the place will not be England

for Armagh see Amritsar
for boogie see bhanghra
for Bangor see Bangor
for cough see catch
for cool see coal
for coal see Cale
for sward see sword
for shit see seams
for craic see crap
for cough see cwrw
for lough see lung
for query see quarry
for whistle see whippet
for bog see big
for tay see tea
for praise see pies
for Toaiseach see tshirt
for Yeats see yeast
for true cross see mosque
for Morrison see Morriston
for Muldoon see Maldwyn
for hurling see Gwylim
for error see earlier
for temperance see tandoori
for poteen see potency
for Cathal O' Searcaigh see Kashmiri Leek Passanda
for Nuala Ní Dhomhnaill see Radjit ap Singh

ST DAVID'S HALL

After the concert they come out: Dafydd ap Gwilym,
William W. Williams, Williamstown, Sion a Sian,
Ivor Emanuel, Lloyd George, Gelert, Owain Glyn Dŵr,
Mrs Davies Plas Newydd, Wyre Davies BBC
so glad there's no one here to mangle his name.
Some bear programmes like souvenir flags.
Their souls have been enlivened
by po-faced Elijah & enormous cymrectitude:
huge handbags, polyester shirts, those woollen celtic
drapes that make you look like an overweight bat, M&S ties.
They discuss school funding, where to go for supper,
death last week, look there's Alun Michael, disgrace,
that Ron didn't need Clapham we have our own parks,
chi wedi mwynhau, the timpani especially.

And there are the kids, the ones who didn't bother to go in,
unworried about identity, sitting in the bar worse than Cerys,
Welsher than R.S., louder than Iwan Bala.
New Wales unselfishly immersed in the national pastime
alcohol alcohol antipathy antidote,
not mentioned anywhere in the Assembly agenda.
Dim pwynt see bachgen it's like breathing
you don't think, you do it, pwy yw Saunders anyway?
Over the speakers gloriously come the Furries

SOME CHRISTMAS HAIKU

On the moors
The snow caught by grass
No one to see it

Not Christmas holy silent night
But the holiday season
Above the cloud same old moon

Cinio Nadolig
boldly praising Iesu
Menu's in English

In the chapel
Old wood
After so many years still shining

Through the dense firs
Light of a wrecked car
Burning

Outside the building society
A man in a Santa suit
And three women smoking

Nadolig heddwch
half of Wales don't care
Other half can't pronounce it

Sound of retching
Three men in an empty street
Crushing lager cans

Nadolig sale sign shop closes
can't wait
for it to open again

Sod dolig this bunt
mmm do it dunit
don matter do it again

DINAS POWIS

South Wales unknown offbeat ramble
number sixteen has us
full boots and clog mud
emerge on the main
fairway of Dinas Powis golf
club men in yellow socks
and diamond pattern jumpers
with Pringle on the breast the
trail is manicured grass and
dark looks but
this is an ancient way we
stride righteous in our
luminous waterproofs
cross the green push through
the hedge two fences ploughed
ground thick copse later the path
peters totally back of a bungalow
PRIVATE sign and a fiery
watercourse throw the offbeat
guidebook into the unknown brook

WATKIN PATH

up the crowded slog
which four-foot fat
Manon did two years back so
I daren't complain a gent in
tweeds bravely pulling on a
woodbine stopped on the
zig-zags sun no rock
painted Bashō haiku but
the train on Crib y Ddysgl
out of Dali   the summit
clog gross llanbuggery white
heeled handbag the way
off retaining grace is Sir Edward
Watkin's 1890 vertical heartstop
descended jellyleg vertigo
and blind then the long miles to
Gladstone's great ice-polished
slab where he once addressed the
people of Eryri on justice and I
lie for half an hour to see if
the shaking stops   sky still there
dry blue and most of it still up

BEN LOMOND

Up steep Ben Lomond nothing
like the Gribyn left boot
full of mud at the outset the
wind picking up no Asda bags
anywhere locals descending in
full mountain gear me breathy Skywalk
Suede Easywear cleats and my
hands frozen.
The tree line breached gale
whacking toggles face roughed by
the velcro I stop
a huge red beard who
says och lad without crampons
yr dead sinking his
skipole into rising snow lots
of sky a couple of climbers
like dark sheep and a blizzard beyond
me slid into a gully sod ice trousers no
thermos a Glasgow Tourist Department
Days Out Guide and a Rennie Mackintosh
label pkt of shortbread   page three
an easy family walk   I'll tell them that
at the Cranston tea-rooms when I get back.

BUILDING BUSINESS

At the morale-build conference
for middle-managers at a hotel so big
the atrium has clouds we sit at the back
in our suits with our badges saying
My Name Is Peter and our bottles of
Malvern Water. The overhead on the
platform says *Love The Customer* we are
looking but everyone here is staff.
The Chairman has an associate taking the
names of those at the back. The overhead
reads *You Only Succeed By Being In Front.*
The Chairman is saying
Change Is A Rocket,
Innovation Is The Way and
Win Or Die.
This man has a
way with words.

The guy next to me, my rival at Copiers,
has a list on his lap headed
Things I Want To Shove Up
The Chairman's Arse.
It goes:
Umbrella Handle, Toothbrush Holder,
Two Bars of Soap, Frozen Pig's Tail,
Cattle Horn, Flashlight, Snuff Box,
Wire Spring, Salami, Mortar Pestle,
Kilo of Peas, Vegetarian Burger,
Pool Cue, Kenwood Kitchen Mate, Zucchini,
402 Stones, Toner Bottle, Axe Handle.
I ask him why the Toner?
We make that, he says, signing
my name at the bottom
of the list and handing it
to the collector of topics
for that afternoon's open session.
The chairman is leaning forward
uncharacteristically ranting:

If we don't hit target soon all our
arses are going to be on the line, he says.
I slide out to hotel reception and
ask if they have any spare toner.
Best to be prepared.

GETTING THROUGH THE AGENDA

It's morning. At the meeting I can't seem
to make my mouth work. No one else is
affected. They all talk in fervent streams.

The meeting is so engaging that by Item 3
I'm asleep with my eyes open so but no one can tell.
Years ago at an Arts Management brainstorm boredom
drove me to assembling Airfix Kits on the table edge.
Plastic glue stuck the agenda to my sleeve and
being the arts no one mentioned it. Creativity.
But this is real business, different I guess.

At Item 15 someone proposes that we should agree and
everyone's hand goes up. For something to do I put mine up too,
I've run out of paperclips to unwind.
The man next to me clacks his
briefcase catch says *the train* and goes.
I could have done that, now can't.

By Item 20 my agenda margin is a Maori tattoo and I have
my pen standing like a tree on my notepad's edge. In the dark
far corner the accountant is in Mahayana meditation, or dead.
There are ravens cawing in the chairman's voice and
sea sponges drifting in my head.

At Item 30 I am stretched out to avoid back contact with
my chair. There are 506 grain marks on the table.
They pass me a sheet which asks my expenses.
It has all led to this.
You can smell the sweat as we
stand hauling suit jackets over crushed shirts.
The dark sky will gleam in our headlamps
as we chase it home.
We have made great progress.

My mouth says this,
how the hell does it know
o yes.

WISDOM OF AGE

It's the end of the line in my
mother's beige living room. The
sun is across the floor in dancing
spikes. She's weeping under the faded
print of two chrysanthemums. No tears
just the despair of age.
A fuse has tripped, she's clicked the
light switch until her fingers burn.
Nothing works. She's told me and god
and me again down her black, heavy
phone. Why is the world like
this? What have I done?
Now, together we must face the
faulty future – me standing there with
my yellow screwdriver and
my poultice of fuse-wire,
her with her poor hair
and her need which
clings to us both until we keel
wishing that wisdom would help
but knowing it can't.

THE ONLY BOOK LEFT IN THE HOUSE

In the bottom of my mother's bedside cabinet,
my father dead for a decade, her in care,
I come across the only book left in the house
bar a 1930s' Methodist Bible and
a crumpled catalogue for Green Shield Stamps.

This one, below the cream mix of anodyne
underwear and anonymous cloths,
is brown-wrapped and as discrete as you can
make a Penguin with its distinctive width.
It could be *The Iliad* but it's *Lady Chatterley*.

They must have queued for this at the town's one
bookshop after the steamy trial and the roaring
reports in the Daily Sketch. They poured across its
overtness until bored by its rambling dark country
tang slipped it here among the smalls.

There is little evidence elsewhere of great lit
seeping in on the back of the sensational.
A copy of *Reveille* wrapping some shears.
A Guide to The Great Orme. In the garage a brittle bag
protecting my first poem, pathetic and proud,
published in a magazine where you paid to get in.
My mother showed this to all the neighbours.
I read it again now and wince at the naivety.
Lawrence and I, we define a life.

SPENDING MONEY IN SOVIET RUSSIA

On the steps of the thousand-bed Ukraina,
a Stalin Hilton which looks like Battersea Power Station
a guy with cardboard shoes slides from the dark
and whispers the East-Europe leitmotif,
Change money? For what, I wonder. I've already
queued in Gum, a vast Harrods in greyscale,
to scavenge their stack of 5000 unwindable watches,
entered the gleaming Kutuzovsky Prospekt
to view their empty cabinets.
On what would I spend these endless roubles?
He coughs in his collar and slides
his hand-back upwards under his outstretched chin.
What is this deviant gesture?
This Cyrillic hand signal means drink.

Could I manage more Moskovskaya vodka to top the
litres already plied me by my Writer hosts?
Could I cart further gallons through customs in my
Western knapsack?
Not a chance

I slip our man a hand of British brown coin
(Japanese guidebooks advise their readers to
throw these away as crap) plus a copy of my
concrete poetry which he slides
surreptitiously into his battered mack.
Da, he says, and goes.

When I return inside the hotel desk-clerk
announces in gleeful English that
"British paper now arrived.
Here real news from your Wales country.
Stop homesick. Wondrous prospect."
After two weeks of booklessness and reading
my wallet I smile expectantly.
She hands me *The Daily Worker.*

COOKERY LESSON

You swede thing, lettuce go,
to marrow it'll all be spinach.
Grasp the day my radish,
we can salsify our lust with pimentos.
Land of blanched veg and small fruit
no rhubarb in public.
My laxton is superb
and your broccoli purple.
Do not worry I have some kumquats.
Steam in moderate heat.
If anyone asks there are only
two things in the world
that smell like this
and one of them is haddock.

WELL-PROPORTIONED PANORAMA

Alive in Wales is informed
At dusk of an opposite blood
That has been going about as a manufactured savage sky product,
Dying our immaculate books.
They all have understood their expenses
It has to be said.
Above the noisy tractor
And the virile bee of the machine.
It is the dissension in the drink that they ache,
Vibrant with acclimatised arrangements.
You can live with peasants
At last in Wales.
There is the linguaphone for example,
Consonants that have the candy
Strange to the ear,
There is the shout in the Gogledd this evening
Similar to owls on the moon,
And a heart shitting in the bushes,
Calming the polyester of the hills.
It has never been the present in Wales,
And the future
Is a racy bodice-ripper stolen from the past,
Fragile with Vernacular
A colon-exhaled nibble mansion
With imposing ghosts
Misunderstood exploits and men
Of infirm person,
Cancelling their traverses,
To widdle on the dictionaries of a polyurethane song.

*[A poem by R.S.Thomas after traversing the text several
times through translation software.]*

BUSINESS

Big is better.
Focus on survivors.
Analyse because invention is so unpredictable / be unpredict oh.
Disturbers must go.
Decide to decide to decide the decision then control.
Tidy and controlled and complex and controlled.
Make one then two.
People are only factors weed the problem go away. Make three.
Over-reward the deciders burn the wood and it's bigger big is better.
Check and look and check and read the figures they're a novel.

One and one and one and one and one and one and one and one
that's a smart boy.
Don't understand but understand no sleep.
Sleep and you'll die. This isn't money this is life.

(sourced from Tom Peters and Robert H. Waterman's "In Search of Excellence")

THE PLUMS

This is just / even / legally / solicitously / almost /
joustingly / about / perhaps / finally / to say

That I have / hidden / recited / sat on / thrown down /
tinned / bellowed / shone / farted / the plums

Which you were / they were / I was / even / possibly tomato /
sparkling / tart-like / bagged / frozen / keeping

For supper / songtime / sunset / sinister practises / sex /
sestina making / sorbet / stippling / stroking / smarting /
simmering / sausage filling / fruity sliver /

They were so delicious / Davies / dozens / delicate / determined /
deep sea / Celine Dion dodecahedron / and sweet

So sweet and / so seasonably / sea-like / sustaining /
and scornfully cold

BUS STOP

On the way to this bus stop I pass a pole where the painted mark once indicated a fare stage: 25% increase to board here (No 30 Newport stops for pick-up only not alighting); walk 600 yards, save, become healthier. For short periods the advertisements were on the fronts of yellow, hard-polypropylene, pole-fixed wastebins. Short because these litter savers were prone to total melt when accommodating unstubbed cigarette butts or still flaring England's Glory. Revenue declined. After the Orange vs. Blue wars with Orange victorious the slogans reappeared first as spot-welded printed-plate (too small), then full-sheet paper brush-pasted (graffitiable) and finally AO total-wall wipe-clear perspex with recessed screws. The revenue offsets capital depreciation, further rain shelters earn more. We all win. The new stops are magnificent – body rest points on revolving hinges like swing seats, unshatterable windows, box-ends against wind tunnel, timetable (weekdays, Saturdays, sun & bank holiday) plus pictures. Like home. The big Orange shows up almost totally obscured with painted copy. There's a winding panel on there somewhere says Depot and a driver with a mad look like axe-man Jack Nicholson in The Shining. I have no idea where the depot is and anyway the bus doesn't stop. According to the timetable that was the 11.07 last run. The shelter end-panel advertises Atgofiadau. I walk home planning to buy some.

GOOD NAMES FOR CATS

Joseph Alfred Bradney, Brenda Chamberlain, Wiliam Cynwal, Cynfrig ap Dafydd Goch, David David Davies, Arthur (King), Thomas Firbank, Harri Gwynn, Hywel Foel ap Griffri ap Pwyll Wyddel, Syr Hywel Ddu o Fuellt, Kingsley Amis, John Osmond, Barry John, Margaret Roberts, Louie Myfanwy Thomas, Ivor Waters, Clywedog Watcyn, William William Williams, William ap William William Williams, W. Williams, Prys ap Williams, Nigel Jenkins, William Jenkins, Herbert Williams, Debra Blackhurst, William Blackhurst, Gordon Houlston, Brian James, Sarah Merry, Peter Perkins, David Thomas, Jim Regan, Van Morrison, Ted Rowland, R. Goodway, Sioned Puw, John Morris, Nicholas Edwards, Peter Walker, David Hunt, John Redwood, William Hague, Ron Davies, Rod Jedwood, R. Miming Natwood, Lynda Thorne, D. Salter, Shirley Bassey, Max Phillips, Tomas Jones, Thomas Brain, Tapper Jones, Harry Holland, Geraint Talfan Davies, Pei, John Jones, J. Jones, J. Johns, T. Mills (piano), Daniel Abse, Leonora Britto, M. Stevens, A. Howell, Hwyl Howell, I. Thomas, & Tabby

FOOD DEPRIVATION AND LIFE EXPECTANCY

Assuming that you are at all concerned you should think very seriously about the social and psychological implications of living many decades as an elderly person. Do you rll? En 100 ssk. If rmmmm is nn vig vig oldolder older extremely difficult. For example is 'undernutrition without malnutrition' womb achi ngly ness ll calor ll ns ns? Cd b. You w dn t nnn rr wor encid. Th essential f at tuf lof dic mm. Overt psychotic increase the large huge canvas yes indeed. Kp bdy ww ww. Kp bdy ww ww way. Dn. Amts of components even material decrs. Nut, fruit and veg, tt ny 1200 sk. We are generally programmed to age and eventually di. Mmm. Mxi mmmm. Vn ills lllllls ills cd b undertake ndert box buried vn vs burn instead. Gen lly yy sk hope his ths is ss kf ven the older wmhmm cra crik crok skn scll l. With a hammer. Carbno ss yik perso ven wei dn own d ev the weird cd wei too long. Card. S won ss t. Drk drk lls evn this deprivation thn evn this.

Nml ven free accs ess cs ess ood ood. Lll twenty-seven rim bo drnk illus ease pain. Cd free veg verg puls n fbr for months. Not enough egg. Survery dark dk k dark n sss. Eat less for most of your life. Lot less. Best.

From REAL CARDIFF (2002)

MEWN

coke legals shirt-tail bay boy whoppa cwpan cymraeg Korea siapan mall
sneakers ice devils 5.00 am suit and armband Koran pack glass massaged
glass fat arse plane crap train Tom Jones Iwan Bala Cerys anything dragon
bluebirds flags café money Mermaid Mallard's Reach Flying Trout
Hemmingway Heaven Bosun's Avenue Atlantic Wharf Leisure Village
Glass Waving slate stacked the Russell Goodway Memorial Roundabout
cycle way speed stripe pile of bricks euro-time multi-screen disposable
glory future proof young assembling assembly absolutely.

MAS

Victoria Park coal and steel mild pale Harlech Sophia Shakin Dunleavy
night Philanderer Jim Callaghan corporation west of England red light
Vic Parker aright skip ship matey pint of sarsaparilla 10.30 Spanish club
afternoon valley day Portland stone Metal Street black mortar Taff Vale
Tom Jones Shirl walking Crockherbtown Caribbean red light bike over-
time Christian marching salvaged beam engines Pink Floyd flood trolley
Estonian Polski coffee bar Italiano fog Welcome to Cardiff General that's
the Pearl Building do not walk in the gutter sorry.

WRITER'S GUIDELINES

A pamphlet of poems and a hard-backed novel will accelerate
    at the same speed when you chuck them down a stairwell.

Fiction always ends

Tall writers are older than short ones

Poems grow spontaneously overnight

You can learn most of what you need from a book simply by
    carrying it about.

Fixing buggered metre is as easy as unplugging the sink

Say hello often enough and you'll soon be famous

Write by saying you have.

Make it up

Why not.

TEXT MESSAGE FROM FFYNNON DENIS

Fnd tp Rth Pk Lk
a pnd h2o seep
sme bbbls &
1 duck
trfic cne & frdg.
put drp on eye in
strng drzz -
mke sgn of crss
dnt do a thng

LIFTING

Chew string. Make it as wet as you can. Lay it along the gutter of your chosen book. Put it next to the printed plate you wish to remove. Replace the book on the shelf. Leave quiet for five minutes to enable the saliva to penetrate the paper. Return and slide the plate out. It will detach soundlessly. All art should be free.

Wear a greatcoat. Large, scarf, double breasted, flap and hang. Books can slide in easily from shelves at waist height.

Bags. Never underestimate the two handled tote, open zip, half full of compressible clothes. Drop in the paperbacks. Crush them down.

Fall over, diversion. Accomplice clears the shelf.

Fall over, diversion. The stock you shower from the shelf with you ends up under your coat.

Fall over, diversion. The books you have in your briefcase they help you carry to the door.

Insult the counter staff. They will not want to continue eye contact. Help yourself.

Take the book to the cash point and insist it's yours, given to you as a present in error, you have it anyway, you don't want it, it's a mistake, can you have a refund, this once, no receipt sorry, you are a regular customer, say so, even if you are not, smile, yes yes, smile again, they flicker, the money waveringly comes at you, take it and go.

Remove the £80 art coffee-table masterwork from the display shelf and boldly march with it out through the entrance. Such audacity. Half the time no one will notice you've gone.

Complain. Makes you innocent.

Run. You are usually faster.

Not at closing time or first customer. Join the crowds mid-morning, lunch-time, 3.00pm Saturday afternoon.

Oh the brilliance of the Christmas run up and heavy rain.

Oriel prosecuted. The manager could manage 6 minute miles. He could then. Someone once made off with 400 postcards showing the grave of Dylan Thomas. Oriel got them all back.

BUILT ON A LOST RIVER
HOW DO YOU KNOW

drain covers lift after
rainfall

cellar fills

leaf

trees

moss

turf declining

map

memory

shapes of Africa rising
on the walls

bronchitis, ague, fever

your daintie nostrills
(in so hot a season, When
every clerke eates
artichokes and peason,
Laxative lettus, and
such windie meate)

surface ponding

overnight shoes
so white in the morning

the ghosts in the corridor

your bones
how they ache and swell
after storm

yes

the sound

EAST CARDIFF

The white wall was much longer. The number of
books in the study make the beams creak. The
gunera reaches for heaven.

The churchyard was a hill fort. Iron age ghosts inside
the circular walls. The river dried. The basement
of the Churchhouse still floods at high tide.

Dannie Abse in the gardens scratching his name. Rawlins White
pulling mackerel from his henges in the Rumney River.
Death by pestilence not heart attack. Water in the
land like blood.

Residents confuse riot with litter. Complain. The Gardens full
of polystyrene. Arm rest gone from the benches. Milestone
end of Four Elms Road rain wasted.

Shifts: Rath. Roarch. Rhuth. Raz. Reurch. Roarth. Reith.

The sea wall translated into MIME format.

Pengam full of burned out German planes. Orange
brick. Persimmon. Wimpy. Tucker. Goods yards.
Unweathered aspect covered with sunset fire.

On the site of the Roath Brick works, reen, tidefield,
clay bog. Raped and left half-naked. Welts.

Bird swarm. Redshanks. Dunlin.
The causeway east crosses two bridges. Evidence in the
mud of men smoking. Clay back to clay.

No one east of the pottery owned a piano. Songs sung
as the Roman road sank, stones gone for walls, passage
now untraceable: Hit The Road Jack; The Road I'm On;
On The Road Again; Take Me Home, Country Roads; Ride
That Tiger; The Long And Winding; Ride Me Ptolemy;
Maximus, Show Me How To Get Home.

The books weigh

We do not read them
We look at them
We shine their spines

The correct Roath had no women two Jews hardly any
history.

I take the books in a station wagon to the landfill and dump
them. Poems that tried hard. Hovered. Hung on for thirty years.
Staple rust. 64 mil pulp.

Roath limits: remember; found; list; told about; posted.
Loan words lead nowhere. There is nothing under the
soil in the garden bar clay and clay and finally shale.

The Ratostabius River (unknw)

Great house with its obtrusive, added columned porch. Yard
and stables converted to rooms where the dead get laid.
Grounds eroded by roads. Bus lane through the gatehouse
the smithy under strip development then flats.

Greyhound.

Love, desp
alley

Cymrectitude blind.

Coal was a bacillus staining. Dock
line in a ruck of trees. Gone.

Cinder foundation, I'm told. Black mortar. Red brick.

Key words: Colchester, Dorchester, Albany; Marlborough;
Waterloo; Sandringham; Kimberly; Blenheim; Harrismith; Alma.

Rain from the west, sheet and sheen. I dig down to look
for them, the cinders. Orange clay like a lifted body part.

A kidney, maybe.

A stomach lining. A liver.

Hole watches me, empty.

Winks.

Then water fills it up.

CARDIFF ARTS (OLD)

Wall hanging, dralon,
terylene, nylon,
lady with fish, fag-packet poodle,
Magistrates Court, cannons,
flowerbed feathers, rug's + carpets,
shipbits, dragons, daff on watertower,
St David's #2 man dancing,
embroidered rendition of miner's lamp,
print of elephant, glass fish, cart horse,
seascape sunset, Prince of Wales,
olde English script Roof Repairs,
Thatcher watercolour Con Club
City Road, Queen Street Xmas
illuminations (July), bus as loaf
of bread, haircut (Rhodri), all fountains,
Andrew Vicari public absence, metal bollocks
city hall, sloped brick main station,
flock wallpaper, rose beds, Attention This Vehicle
Is Reversing, rhif dau osgwelwch yn dda,
Oriel (closed), wall thing in the Castle Roman
Gallery, have you seen this, didn't think so.

A LIBERAL VERSION OF THE PENARTH SEA ANGLING CLUB LIST OF PENARTH PIER FISH

Bass
Coalfish
Cod
Conger Eel
Dab
Dib
Dob
Dogfish
Darkfish
Doodlefish
Esplanade Knickers
Flounder
Fillet
Mullet
Mallet
Moosh
Plaice
Prick
Pollack
Plop
Poor Cod
Dreadful Wallop
Pouting
Spitting
Moaning
Whining
Getting Your Hair Off
Rocklings
Rollings
Silver Eel
Sausages
Soul

R&B
House
Handbag
Adrodd
Welsh Grey
Grecian 2000
Whiting

from THE WELSH POEMS (2006)

FOLD

We (us) (I) (you) were (weren't) (won't) (will) a (the) (this)
people (pointed sticks) (prime numbers) (purple patch) taut
(tired) (tiled) (tight as fists) for (from) (frightened) (foaming)
war (wet fish) (wet fist) (wet fear); the (those) (these)
hills (hovering) (hollow) (high) (high) (high) (heated)
(hardened) were (will not) (can not) (can) no
(none) (neither) (normal) harder (holding) (heaving)
(happy as barber's poles) (hard hosts) (home)

I (we) won't (will) the (those) (that) pointed
(printed) (prattle) stick (stack) (steaming) (coal) (coal)
tired (tilted) (hilltop) (hold) from (fear) (fear) (fear)
(fear) (fear) (refute) wet (wash-off) (westerly) (unwound)
those (this) (these) hovering (unheated) (unworn)
(unbilleted) (unbound) will not (can't) none
(no more) holding (fingertip) (finger-stall)
(finger-push) (thrust) look up (look up)
unshaped (unsure) (uncertain) (unable) like us
(fold) (fold) (fold) folded (fold).

NO BIKE

I have been speaking at my door with the distraught woman who has let her daughter get lost. I am playing Mendelssohn's Violin Concerto in here and feel like I am gliding up a highway in the sun. The woman says her child – you know her, the one with the pink bike and its little outriders – was in the park, went to the park, peddled past here, came up this road, along this path, this way, you saw her smiling, you did. I have been deep in the music and my mind full of wide spaces I tell her I have not I am sorry I shake my head. The woman has on a white blouse with a button missing and straggle hair that's been clipped ragged where it brushes her chest. Her shoes are flat and their leather is scratched. She twists her hands into each other. She looks back. Along the road there is no girl, no bike. I can't tell her anything. She has brown arms and a bangle. She'll turn up. I was with Mendelssohn. The street is hot. The music soared. She is burning, this woman. Her face is melting. All of it, it's coming off. For comfort I remind myself that in other places across the world there are worse fears in the faces of the destitute and the dying. Worse than this. I look at the woman again. Long and slow. No, right now, there are not.

PUTTING IN THE WINDOW

(after Tom Leonard)

Glazunov's Double Concerto
Mozart's C minor Glazing Bar

INTERVAL

Rossini's Stabat Drip Strip
Mendelssohn's Violin Serenade in Soft Putty

Encore: Mahler's Tenth Lintel

PAINT

Violent White
Azure Eyepatch
Winter Arse
Gurgling Sands
Underarm Crush
Blueberry Sandinista
Tropical Testosterone
Sunkist Yellow Underpant
Vanilla Vertigo
Mango Vagina
Warm Topsoil
Duodenum Jade
Fresh Acne

What is the maximum number of times
you have had to repaint the
wall below the dado?

Seven.

HISTORIANS

Historians' output has increased
is increasing
a strict regimen might save us
ought to be diminished
corpulence useless
threatens the vital organs
much of it waste.

A strict regimen
and ought to be diminished
vulgarisations bloat bookshelves
threaten the vital organs
hypertrophy with learning
of learning with hypertrophy
of bookshelves with bloat
much of it is corpulence.

Academic fat clogs the bibliographies
and threatens the vital corpulence
is increasing and ought and otherwise
much of it imposes a starvation
much of it a strict taxpayer
ought to be bloat.

Revolted by the useless corpulence
we need much of it
writers who take pride and
writers who take pride and
writers who waste
patrons and taxpayers
and vulgarisations
Academic fat clogs the bloat
strict history ought to float

We need much of it
vital historians' corporations
taxpayers, bibliographies,
learned bookshelves and bloat
writers who take pride and
ought to be diminished.

the bloat and the vulgarisations
writers who take pride and
reviewers who take prisoners
writers who take pride and
reviewers who take prisoners
writers who take pride and
reviewers who take prisoners
writers who take pride and
reviewers who take prisoners
writers who take pride and
reviewers who take prisoners
writers who take pride and
reviewers who take prisoners
writers who take pride and
reviewers who take books

Much of it is waste
the historians ought the they then
slipshod
oh yes apoplexy
and how they
clog clog and bloat

The output they h'm
might might might
slip sl
The historians then will be vital
increase increased the they them
the historians
will write about it
yes they will.

RHAI CANEUON CYMRAEG

Os gallaf helpu rhywun

Disgyblion Iesu Grist

Er cof am fuwch o'r enw Molly

Cowboi bach tŷ ni

Dos draw Moses

Lisa lân

Caru Cymru

Titw Tomos las

Llongau Caernarfon

Pentre bach Llanber

Hen Feibl Mamgu

Dyma gariad fel y moroedd

My Hen laid a haddock

F'anwylyd f'anwylyd

Hen lwybr y mynydd

Cofio o hyd

Iesu Iesu rwyt ti'n ddigon ('Clawdd Madog')

Beth sydd o'i le

Un fendith dyro im ("Bo Diddley")

Gwely gwag

'Sdim eisiau dweud ffarwel

Hei Ho Noni No

Slingwr gwn ydy Meic Stevens

Mae'r llais yn galw

Gymru lân gwlad y gân

Gymru lân gwlad y two tongues

Gymru lân gwlad y bobl mewn oed

Gymru lân hand in the till

No arabs in Blaenau Ffestiniog ("Land of Hope and Glory")

Seren seren pull a fish from your bottom

Y deryn du a'i blufyn sidan

Ffidl ffadl

Titrwm tatrwm

Totrwm tylli tô

Rhwng Bethesda a'r groes (Cymysgiad clwb)

Y Bugail Tonyrefail

Blow The Wind Southerly

Rhondda Is Where My Heart Is

Swing That Hammer (Cân Serch)

Swing That Hammer (fersiwn R.S.Thomas)

Swing That Hammer (Meredydd Evans a'i fand)

Ei di'r deryn du?

Porthcawl Co-operative Society Rock n Roll Mambo

Once More With Feeling

Yn boeth fel tân

That's enough

LITERATURE

There was hardly a ripple on the water.
Difficult to get a foothold
in the green fluted jar.
Wales is a boar's head
Not that any sneer I was going to make
    would hurt her.
Cadwaladr Tomos. Postman. Farmer,
    boatman, builder.
Calloused heels had worn holes in the linen sheets.
Read these people? Carn find their books.
Most were metal sheet, painted deacon red.
Cathleen drunk and more.
The chapel packed. Deacons, deacons,
miners, faded reds.
The colliers had set their dotty lamps. Lenin
and Lloyd George. Lamps and fire. Ezra.
Big Jim. Ianto. Mishter Cadeirid. Robert
buckling his belt and striding off down the
Road swinging his trap and his
rabbits and humming the Old Hundredth.
People making their way to the chapel.
The mill stream. A young hurricane.
Riding north surrounded by oak woods.
Voices empty as an upturned bucket.
Good it is, and honest. Words they are.
And free. Run and write, is it?
The Big Man calls you to account.
For novelists, Mr Walford had no time.
He had never met one and would never
do anything to favour their existence.
Hogyn spotless Machynlleth rain dark
egg flagon Tegwen hell no siarad
central cleansing lettuce lecture lettuce
leaning left-over lumps lumpen
shoutin somethin bleedin somethin
somethin soon somethin
Adrenalin has turned me skin to sparks.

HOW

Names of those near him lots of some who have influenced him heroes nomdeplumes ffugenwau never alphabetical to get a rhythm drop the forename invent and substitute mangle insert wild cards loose-cannons unknowns very knowns set parenthesis (around) occupations (author) achievements instruments (piano) invented and real drop vowels tighten up tpwrtr kynrds hrt mntr like jazz bnd intrmnts cr pts (xhst) spd mkrs drgs cffne vslne slip slop second half left off. (scnd hf lft f). Descriptors gouged up as overkill then raked through into letter groups. Staccato. Scatter. Sentence end words gathered from his great works and laid out like poms or prim prose, cloud combs, rakes, riddles, mesh filters, sticklebacks. Punctuation dropped gathered letters set in alphabetical groups, strained external mix. Pages from pulp novels. Random lifts from scientific texts. Parts of the text erased fugitive lost. Return to the names of the influenced shuffled and scratched. The revealed accumulated structure could be further distorted but is not. No Ouvroir de littérature potentielle novelmaking. Pommes. Pims. Perms. Touchstones are important. He uses the formulae to parse fragments of reality out of the fog. Strings of pearls. Lights. Poor lights. Leaked battery lit. Damp. Bulbs clouded. But lights.

Probably the most important realisation was that the ear could lead the voice. Hear the distortion and then mimic it. Follow the pale traces of syllable bumping. Pick the uplift as the list rattles towards its conclusion, its inevitable and unemotional end. The signals embed themselves and reproduce like amoebae. Cells multiplying ( ) ( ) ( ) list and reorder. Take the lyric apart and see how it stands up. Unbolt the sonnet and let the parts roll in the dirt. There's dirt in all this. Sticks to everything. Don't clean it off. Most important thing in the world.

INSTEAD OF WRITING

Fix the toner gain immense satisfaction ring the creditcard company the shop the loose the way the door hangs. Strung. Mostly anyway there's death to contend with. Skin erupting with distemper discolouration dysfunction don't care. Lower teeth gone to hell. Pain in the bladder. Cartilage worn. Things stuck and leaking. Energy enough for one burst then you're fucked. Cobbing, Redgrove, Wantling, Glyn Jones with one arm. There is nothing new in this world, the clocks spin, the dust arrives, the dust never went

I teach the method avoid slowing. Get the action noted as near the action as possible. Don't let time intervene. Time fat slug enveloper deadly smoke. But it's not the real enemy the best enemy the biggest most deadly. That's instead. Anything other. Pick the lint from your trousers. Instead of writing you fix the broken oil in clean lift move the furniture stare through the glass at the watch the window snowstorm rain flecks of light. These patterns that roll in. Arms out like Leonardo like crosses like stars like Catherine wheels. They dazzle. They disrupt.

Glyn said you listen sometimes you stop sometimes you pick things up. Wantling felt the pain and pushed it. Redgrove noted and scratched. Cobbing picked and smeared and slashed. Outside there's synchronicity diversion dismay and great showers of falling might. The poems stick like dead babies. Not born. Left to shrink and darken. They emerge if ever they do years on as smears and flecks and lines of dust.

It's a dark life this endless search for light.

MARDY MAERDY

Maerdy communi hung. 30 meetings in support of the Spanish Republic's stru against fascism. Stri. The family, now, is an epitome of. ke. Side. Sl. ritle. Political struggle. Jones. Jones. Rprnt official. Twice.

Mardy farm. Flatlands no memory of valley sides.

Ballard airport. Wrecked Cessna nose dived near the sea wall. Reclaimed marsh and tidefield. Drainage reens. Sluice. Hedge. Scrape across the wet soil where the wing had turned. No evidence of fire or death. Gulls and crows.

The deserted microprocessor plant sits beyond, behind a line of limestone boulders. Landed here from Mars. Five years empty, green glass low rise, its vacant workshops and unused offices lack even regular trash. No balled papers or whorls of dust in their corners. At the far end of the car park, huge and ordered, spaces numbered and without a single oil stain, two ponies nose among the grass verges. There'd been youngsters here earlier, twelve year-olds, space-helmeted, buzzing on squat yellow motorbikes, but they'd gone. In the entrance hall, wood fronted reception desk, discrete lighting, space and calm, stood a glass-cased model of the plant itself. No name plate. None ever fixed. No finger marks. Architects' miniature trees sprouted where in the larger world there were none. Artics leaving full of stock. In the real loading bays, a line of silent grey plastic mouths, nothing moved. Cold war without weapons. No uniforms or guns. Crow on the powerline. Wind. A siren drones in the distance. Break in to steal nothing. The wail rises and falls like a migraine pulsing. Consciousness shut down here as if an experiment to stay awake forever had gone horribly wrong.

I find a guard making tea in a hut beside rising barriers that rarely move. His copy of The Sun and boxed sandwiches are the only things on the vast control desk. An intercom that connects to silence. Switches for lights that never come on. A 3K fan heater filched from somewhere blowing. Didn't work, he tells me. Nothing down here does. The Koreans gave up. Then it was the Chinese but they never came. He's written something onto a chart but the mould has got it. Fossil. He smiles. What's the place called? Mardy. Reen and sluice and farm.

Drenewydd, Pencoed, Broadway, St Brides fen-banks, Horsecroft, Summerway, Hawse, Back-fen Moor, Catchwater drain, bog oak, Black Moor.

Mardy the Reeve's House. The bailiff. Cavalry horse bones. Salt. Inter tidal blanket.

Rmns failed in. Valley. Ownr. Lewis Jones, barely 40, died in 1937. Maerdy closed in 1984. Mardy 2006 never opened at all.

NOTHING IS NEW

It's been a long day, waiting for Osmond Oshmail Osaman Ormondold Ormond. I'm in the front bar of the Conway. Fug and warm. Half a pint. Worried. I'm a young man. An incredibly young man. Bright. Skin. Hair. Eyes. My poem is in my pocket foolscap typed three pages nothing I don't know searching hefty little mag Henri easy about being something going somewhere words being young. John said bring it it's brought. He arrives in his trademark grey tweedy jacket. Bulbous pockets. Nothing in them. Leather buttons. Tufty hair. This poem he looks at it kindly slowly sort of reads it half takes it in without wincing why don't you take this first part move it to the end put the middle at the start cut up shuffle. Hands in the air in waving demonstration. Can't work. Can't work. We do it. On the table. Text. Beer stains. It can.

The sole Scientific and Magical Colonel of Space. Great rays. Insights arriving while we look away. We don't screw our faces up. We don't tough with the arms out long. We don't consider smoke. We don't let the mind drift or pin sharp or blur. We don't paint anything. We don't talk. We look at each other and it's done.

John says there's nothing new under the sun he was trying these dada rolls and lists and the surrealist nonsense and the way the third mind controls how you write that's god that's what powers this that's been done I've done it did it do it many times. So show me. Gone. Didn't like the results enough abandoned and moved in these other Auden directions care and chivvy, push and press, let the mind go loose then reel it in pin sharp. Moved on.

We drink. Smile. Fold the poem back into the pocket. Think about what you are doing. Did some of that. Did some more. And again.

PUBLISHING

I went to Birmingham with Crow cigarettes and hitching. The cabs were easy and they talked but you didn't have to answer. Crow had the big idea. I thought he had the big idea. The radios would drown most of it. Countryside. Countryside. Countryside. We got there and he showed me his notebook pulp hardback frightening hands. Poms. Baroque serifs in biro. Intertextural illuminated catchword dry pointed. This is it, man. Hands self-tattooed ink smeared dark. The sky is serrated.

There are seven stencils and one typer me on the typer and Crow with a pen scratching his cover. It's loopy. Flying saucers and ghosts and hosts of demons chasing each other across the cosmos. Inside my head, says Crow. Hand on his ear lift it and the angels might stream out. Birmingham air. Combat jackets. Fur. Bottom of jeans embellished with sew-ons. Boots. No bells. Terry Riley Poppy No Good and the Phantom Band. Like the sky same piece repeats and moves it's the same but different it changes doesn't change comes back looks like sky is the sky same again all the time anyway. Crow's poems are medieval indictments of self-loathing full of rage and fury. The world is heavy on inflatable huge burgers bright flat colours white plastic and hope.

We get a hundred copies and wire-staple down the left hand margin. Big floppy foolscap full of immediate energy with most of the text written only hours before print. How you do it. Plastic bags. Poetry man this is real. Crow smiles through his dark beard spiky bits there are teeth in there no one has ever seen Crow's teeth. So we have these poems and somehow the world will change because of it. There's a feeling that the angels are pushing us. Saw Wordsworth on the paths as we came here. Felt Blake in the landscape. Taliesin making the hills vibrate.

They don't sell. We try but they don't. Should have known. There's a woman shifting The Watchtower and she's done thirty just pan-handling across the bar. I've managed nothing. She's big and black dressed and hatted. Earlier age. I'm now. Mod feint soft shoes cords jacket thin tie. Burroughs wore a suit all his life to enable him to fade into the background. The background where the observers stand. Float unseen. Soft hands. Eyes that skim and drift but rarely stick. But in this place doesn't work.

1966 wasn't it? Mitch Ryder Beatles Temptations Wilson Pickett. Juke and cider. Poems in the hands and the idea of poems and the way they flushed up the sky and made the air so pure. Bag of books under the bed. Cardiff unsolds back from the midlands smoke. Crow stayed there. Dope and hedges. Corners. Flat out, man. I am a published writer. Yep. There with the dust whorls and the detritus. Staples rust. Some foxing. Covers mostly intact.

TUNNEL FOG

train space elongated
Doppler horses great grass
poles huts coal signal
pipes carve emulsify gosh

tunnel fog settle
horizon sunlight blind blind
two words half half
dog field water gash

eye space serge surge
vibrate welcome spray spread
oil detritus thermal latch
Severn Tunnel Junct

thi ss eye concip
I wnt ou ite ite ite
conseu fish fi somet
co hard iron cla gg

mordant flake white
layers stream organic
en vibvibvibvibrr
envrr vibrrr rrrrrrrrr

half the book full
start anywhere
mist and light and
hard overheard fragmn

more real tkt sir
manufactured lifted bolt
shone oil once slide
hole hole

hole for swarm dark
for cover tension for
topographical bund for
heart balloon for breath

nte (lost) happened once
nte (lost) happened agai
nte (lost) happened n
result of dope or drunk

sonnet lost property
junction residue purchase
sorry mate fill this
finish piss for sod

next first second third
terminates terminated
start anywhere
linen calculus heat

mem (could)
lines to the horizon
navigator hammer
no need for paper

air (did)

ROUGH SKIN

He'd come on the train all the way back to Cardiff with the ends of his fingers split and the edge of his thumb rough against the side of his chin. A dermatological condition he hadn't yet got to the bottom of. Cellotape and toilet paper kept the blood back, cold cream helped the roughness but he'd need something stronger. Soon. The tunnel had been a flash of dark in two and half hours of rattling grey. When he was a child it was smoke and spark and fear of drowning, water rush, windows dark and rattling, the rough upholstery of the 2nd class compartment seats making marks on the undersides of legs. Wales outside now. Grown into by the land next to it. Accent worn thin from buffeting. Full of rain.

In the hotel where he'd stopped for a drink he was the only thing moving bar Celebrity Big Brother on the mumbling TV. Vodka, no ice they'd run out, cold lemon. Big argument about who should pour the tonic in. Being the customer offered no privileges. Vodka was a package, bottled and flavoured. The paper was full of endings. Half of it filched. Nothing longer than three paragraphs. Sentences so short they felt like his scalp did after he'd razored it. Stabs and shouts. Didn't matter you couldn't remember. Pick up another.

Ends of his fingers sloughing on the strings. Bled. MacSweeney came up the stairs to this bar once in a rare sober moment. Tape of Iris Dement in his bag. Country music nothing about poetry. Bright and red flushed. Hands under the table. Three months later it was a different story. Vodka bottle in the briefcase. Took ten minutes to get the poem scrap paper bundle gaggle out pain creasing ten further a wide avoiding circle then looming back to the text, falling at it, taking the line and stuffing it, half uttered, half swallowed, falling off and back, lurching the verse like an earth remover, taking the top off as a drunken driver would. Crushing it. Blood everywhere. I gave the audience their money back smiling most of them refused. Barry holding me like a brother, hadn't paid him, loved it here, do it again, could he come back? Full of demons he died instead.

The hotel rains. Two shoppers taking tea delivered on a huge tray by a boy in ill-fitting clothes and scratchy neck. Vodka empty. Bookshop on the corner had never heard of MacSweeney. Unstockable. Print to order then in a padded bag despatch to an address where you're out most of the time. No one to sign for it, have to collect. Are these the streets the hipsters were going to take and make their own? Charlie Parker and Robert Johnson. Bob Cobbing and Hughie Green. Edmundo Ros and Bryan Johnson. Barry Mac and those other bastards. Who were they? Did anyone see them off? Pick up my bag. Hands almost had it. Wearing down like a leather shoe sole. Reheeled so many times the place the nails go is buggered. No book. No Mac. Half a newspaper and outside sheets of rain. Where else could I be but home.

TEA ROOM

In the tea room where they'd stopped and the owner had served them egg and bacon on the best china, floral, gold edges, linen table cloth, knives and forks with fish ends and silver salt shaker where the salt flowed had never yet been damp he could imagine his mother. Cobbing liked the far west where time slowed and great gaps emerged into which you could fall. Fissures. Finger ends. Tap the poems. They had tea strong enough to bend spoons, clinking cups, cube sugar, toast. Bentwood chairs. Sunlight. Empty apart from them. Washed up in a Ceredigion dream. Twanging on his big Gretsch Duane Eddy in the background not Bois y Blacbord. Finch tapped his fingers. Cobbing watched the trembling air.

They took the road back in a car that leaked marking its territory as it went like a cat. Cat. Cart. Critch. Kringle Cat. Coot. Cooloop Cat. Can Can Teenadan Can Deeta Canrowtoo Canreeta Canrowtoo Cancreela Crimb Crime Crark Cat. Cob had two one huge with a lazy tongue one black and white with fragile bones so deep down in the fur you knew it had to be old. Sun through the windscreen Cobbing with his winder down like Kerouac Dean Moriarty Cody Pomeray Japhy Ryder high on nothing shouting poems at rising rock water sheep. Uplands getting bigger. Cambrian. Another land.

This was the Cwmystwyth Road that went up through where the Romans once mined lead and the wreck of a more contemporary quarry still sprawled down the hillside on a sea of shale, the road winding through it. They stopped and scrambled. Finch found an iron bolt, the past. Took it. Cobbing piled stones, the present. Left them.

Things he said: monotype, variations, tu to ratu, copierprints, vexation, cataclysms, stills, destructions, reproductions, faulting, symposium, nimbu, movement, plural vague, things you run after but can't catch. Lao Tsu. Pablo Neruda. Marcel Duchamp. Cornelius Cardew. Eric Mottram. Mac Low McClure. Caught on.

The road back took them through forests. High plains. Peat mass. A rare kite swooping. Silent skies like the tops of drums.

TOO LATE

It's too late to bring the book out. The other guy brought his out last week. Doing yours now will make you seem a copycat fellow traveller faker Johnny come lately rider on the coat tails imitator facsimile worker photocopier scanner replicator. How much space do we need? He's whirling through the bookstores on a tide of fame and swooning. What can you do? Can you do anything? R.S. Thomas wasn't concerned when he made his small first one. Whitman sold his from a basket like an itinerant salesman shifting apples. Edgar Poe printed forty and sent them all out for review. No one wrote any thing. He never kept an author's copy. Poetry vanished into the maw. Doesn't matter now. It seems. So the bookstore has flashing lights and his picture large in the window. He's famous for something else. Poetry on its own pulls nothing. Unless you are Seamus. Farmer's Son Wins Big Prize. Legendary Irish newspaper headline.

Do yours now. The weight will lift. Think of titles that can be readily remembered. Ten Lovely Thoughts are useless. Random Jottings are full of fog. Forget the bookshops. Authors just rearrange the displays there to put themselves constantly on top. No one buys anything anyway they just look then go home and order clean cheaper editions on eBay or Amazon. Your book is you in a bright suit and full of colour. You talking with your clear voice and the sun making the lines of your face so handsome. Make the pic of you on the back cover one your mother will be proud of. Young you. Hair and face. Intellectual hand holding your beautiful chin. Get it out now. Purge yourself.

Poems stacked and laid out with great care over margins (space for fingers) and how the titles sit in their fonts, gleaming, and the endings don't stumble lonely onto distant pages. This is having something stuck inside you and calling in help to have a hand down your long throat and pull it up removed. This is arguing for five hours without a stop until she gives in or leaves you. This is digging until the pond is big enough to drown in. This is staying on the line until they put the phone down. This is the gourd vine finally with heavy fruit. Ugly and empty and you can't eat them. In Africa they are hollowed and chickens kept in them. Here they come in packets of thirty, brown paper, cellotaped, bk poms felt penned upside down on each end, stacked under the bed, on all the shelves, front room, half the hallway full. Wonderful. Sitting on the step, copy in hand. Name. Gloss. Colour splash. Blurb. Contents. Poems. Poms. Perms. Hold them. Now.

TORRANCE

Talus tectonic uplift erosion freeze thaw tree-line alluvium fossil image brittle streambed pattern weight joint anthracite great heat carbon felt pen weather chart cloud layer sun su sun sun grassbox. Ley line power chi cloud stream line wool hat flask walkng jkt boots hat ruck. Text in all pockets. Where the lines intersect.

Forest ice fossilized brew brew cultural pressure-release woven into steep pile. Bone near skin. Slow arrival. Talkbox. Skein.

New moon new weather can't find these crushed wet pulp river borne pages dŵr of nadw above boots across two fields buckets. First thoughts most thoughts best thoughts Kerouac Wyatt Whalen Williams Pilcher New York Duncan Open Field Creeley Olsen Black Mountain landscape vastness beyond here snow and ice limestone sink hole precipitation flowing.

Inside lan gua ged oes n't mea nCh opi n's par tic les her ebu tad eep ern eur olo gic alf low Tor ran ced ecl aim ing wit hme ani ngh ang ing his coa tta ils lik ean old dog ack now led geh isb rot her sbu tdo n't bel ike the m man I chatter I prattle must slim this get lean and mean in the line tone and space and margin. Shoes like Woody Guthrie. No boxcars anywhere in the high Neath Valley. Man with a dog. Mist. Dope. Brychan.

Line into the future like a memory.

No grid link, biomass, tubs of alcohol, doors into other worlds

Things he said time is a magma doubts linger in the barrel my attachment is my attachment is my attachment

Weather shapes it all

SWELL

On the high street on a day when the drizzle has been going for hours is best. Take everything you see and swell them. Make them so big they push out and into each other. Shopfronts soft bulging into street furniture pelican lights bent and elongating. Signs tacked up saying Grand Furniture Sale & Computer Day Festival Thousands of Bargains so huge and turned their lettering becomes concrete poetry billboard adverts for Bars and Furns and Ains. All colour bleeding off the edges. Cars ballooned making them like the bulbous 1950s all over again, chrome in glinting streaks, mangling with gargantuan shopping, brown veg like river sludge. Broccoli forests. Orange fire. Health food tablets chalk power and bark scrapings twenty pound for thirty may take a few months for any difference to be discerned heaped like 1968 Paris road cobbles. In this mash an eyebrow. Elbow poking. Some denim lining the bank walls. Clouds of coiffured hair floating. Light despite the contraction of space. Headlamps like suns. Bus bent into a philosophy of how it and its cargo might be. Ideas for love and lust streaming. It melds and bends and ebbs and flows. Push it and it flows.

Round the back in the pub use your pad and get it down. Old pubs are best. Something about the life that's flowed through them reaching you through the seats you sit on. Something about the talk in that air held still by the wallpaper. Something about the passion in the touch of glass. Something about the future never imagined. Something about the now surrounding you like a blanket. Get crisps and nuts for sustenance. This is not Buddhism you can eat them. Pick them. Let them clog your veins. Relax. Fear nothing. Write everything down.

These *Selected Later Poems* follow on from the author's *Selected Poems* which was published at Cary Archard's instigation by Poetry Wales Press in 1987.

3 am. Hinckley Point B nuclear power station is situated near Bridgwater in Somerset, directly across the Bristol Channel from Cardiff. During the late 80s when this poem was written the controversial building of a third Hinkley Point C reactor on the site was a distinct possibility. Hinkley Point A closed in 2000. Hinkley Point B with its two AGR reactors continues to function.

We Can Say That. "Heol y Frenhines" – Queen Street – Cardiff's principal shopping thoroughfare. "Iaith y nefoedd" – the language of heaven (ie Welsh). "Cenedl heb iaith, cenedl heb galon" – a nation without a language, a nation without a heart.

Out At The Edge. Nolton Haven, possibly Pembrokeshire's smallest resort, appears to consist almost entirely of the Mariner's car park.

Mountains: Sheep. Kurt Schwitters' *Ursonata*, a classic dada sound poems of considerable length, is reputed to have been recited by the late George Melly when confronted by a group of muggers. Totally amazed, they let him go unmolested. Zanzibar, an island 6 degrees south of the equator, off Tanzania, is said to be just large enough to take the world's entire human population standing.

Hunting Whitakers. For many years until it was replaced by online resources Whitakers was the booktrade bible which listed all books in print. The 'How To' section was used to mine this found poem.

Dead End. A piece recalling my Mapplewood Court, Llandaff North flat, home of *second aeon* magazine and the place where John Tripp wrote his famous thank you for putting me up note across the wallpaper above the fireplace

Little Mag. A tale of *second aeon* magazine which ran from 1966 to 1974

Dutch. Contrary to its appearance as a found text re-worked this piece is an entirely original composition. Bob Cobbing once remarked that sound poets have learned to imitate unaided the distortions made possible to their voices by magnetic tape. There is an obvious parallel here for found poets.

Ex-Smokes Man Writes Epic. Originally a performance piece for the trio, Horses Mouth, which survives well on the page. The group consisted of Peter Finch along with two other Cabaret 246 writers, Ifor Thomas and Christopher (later Tôpher) Mills.

Hills. A permutational counterpart for Finch's much earlier poem *A Welsh Wordscape* which also begins with a line from R.S.Thomas. This piece originates from the period before the arrival of satellite broadcasting when the West of England TV transmitter was (and still is) situated in the Mendips and reached most of the South Wales coastal belt. Despite the subsequent advent of S4C, the Welsh-medium television channel and the removal to it of every scrap of the language from other stations, most South Wales users kept their aerials pointed across the water apparently preferring the news from Yeovil to reports from Wales.

from *Antibodies.* The *Antibodies* collection appeared in 1997. In it were collected ten years worth of continued innovation. To the long process pieces *The Cheng Man Ch'ing Variations* and *Five Hundred Cobbings* (both extracted from here) were added a whole range of poems derived from permutated findings, adaptations, translations, listings and other structural procedures. The poems sought to resolve Clark Coolidge's question "why make new work when there's so much already around us?". Elements of dada hang on while the pure structures of the concrete poetry movement recede. Ultimately there is always fun.

The Cheng Man Ch'ing Variations. Cheng Man Ch'ing was a Master of T'ai Chi Ch'uan who lived from 1901-1975. He is largely responsible for the popularisation of the Yang style of Tai Chi across the globe. The *Variations* were originally published by Bob Cobbing at Writers Forum.

Five Hundred Cobbings. Bob Cobbing 1920-2002. Britain's foremost sound poet. Performer, publisher, exhibitor, critic, and lynchpin of the UK concrete poetry movement from the 1950s onwards.

Summer School. Sylvester is Dom Sylvester Houedard (1924-1992), the Benedictine monk and concrete poet from Prinknash Abbey famed for his minimalist rendering of Matsuo Bashō's (1644-1694) most celebrated haiku.

All I Need Is Three Plums. Finch is not the first to use William Carlos Williams' note to his wife, "This is just to say" as a starting point for humorous verse making. Kenneth Koch has done so, as have others. Mine celebrates the fruit machine scratch & win charity cards which were sold by the thousands in pubs up and down the country before the advent of Camelot's National Lottery.

The River Finch's companion was the American artist Mags Harries with whom he had worked on the 1995 Swansea Year of Literature Ty Llên Demons Project (see *pg. 65*). The river is the Neath.

RNLD TOMOS. R.S. Thomas's pseudonym in his school magazine was Curtis Langdon. Hart-Davis published his early works. This is an updated version of the poem which originally appeared in *Useful*.

Sonnet No 18. Composed for a special issue of Glyn Pursglove's *The Swansea Review*. This piece reduced Shakespeare's most famous sonnet to its component letters restructured to mirror the form of the original work.

Words Beginning With A This piece was written while Finch was working for HMSO, the Government publisher of the White Paper which eventually established the Welsh Assembly. It was obvious to Finch that the document had been heavily sanitised by Welsh Office civil servants. Key phrases had been edited out. Finch decided to put them back. When the piece was complete the late Robin Reeves at the *New Welsh Review* agreed to publish it. In an attack of cold feet before the issue appeared Finch rang and insisted that the poem appear under a nomdeplume. It did. It was attributed to a Peter French. The magazine noted French as "an experimental poet living in Cardiff".

Irish Guide To Wales Errata. The Toaiseach is the Irish Prime Minister. Cathal O' Searcaigh and Nuala Ní Dhomhnaill are both Irish poets. Paul Muldoon, who has written another *Errata*, and Finch appear to have been bitten by the same bug.

Some Christmas Haiku. Originally commission for an Arts Council of Wales Christmas card in the mid-nineties and for reasons of political correctness not used. Later appeared in Dewi Robert's excellent anthology *Christmas In Wales* (Seren)

Well-Proportioned Panorama. A return to R.S.Thomas's *A Welsh Landscape* used by Finch in the sixties as the basis for his *A Welsh Wordscape.* Two French translation programmes were used, one operating with a larger on-board dictionary than the other. The text was actually traversed from English to French and then back again around thirty times.

The Plums. A return to the famous fridge door note of W. C. Williams.

Bus Stop, and *Good Names For Cats* were written as part of the Llathyard project of 1998. Artists and writers were commissioned to respond to the contemporary culture of promotion and advertising. The results were displayed in poster form on Adshel bus shelters across Cardiff.

Mewn / Mas – In / Out

Text Message From Ffynnon Denis. Ffynnon Denis is one of the lost holy wells of Penylan, in Cardiff. Its waters were said to cure bad eyes.

East Cardiff. The white wall ran from Roath Court up along what is now Albany Road, marking the limits of the Roath Court estate. A small section of the wall still exists, still white, at the southern end.

Cardiff Arts (Old). Before the advent of latter day CBAT-driven public art Cardiff was no visual desert. The Council knew what it liked.

A Liberal Version of the Penarth Sea Angling Club List of Penarth Pier Fish. Derived from the list posted on the end of Penarth Pier.

Fold. (cant)(explain)(can) (might) (read on)

Literature. Lines taken from a range of early twentieth century Anglo-Welsh novels.

Tea Room . Finch's companion was Bob Cobbing.

Torrance. Chris Torrance, open field poet master, Beacon's hermit, lover of ley lines and creator of wonderful texts.

ACKNOWLEDGEMENTS

Some of the poems in this collection were first published in the following anthologies:

Alive In Parts of This Century – Eric Mottram at 70 (North & South 1994) edited by Peterjon & Yasmin Skelt
Best of Asheville Poetry Review 1994-2004 (Asheville 2004)
Between The Severn and the Wye (Windrush Press 1993) edited by Johnny Coppin
Border Voices (Gomer 1999) edited by Geraint Eurig Davies
The Bright Field (Carcanet Press 1991) edited by Meic Stephens
Burning The Bracken (Seren Books 1996) edited by Amy Wack
Christmas In Wales (Seren Books 1997) edited by Dewi Roberts
Everybody's Mother (Peterloo 2001) edited by Linda Coggin & Clare Marlow
Footsteps – An Anthology of Walking in Wales (Gwasg Carreg Gwalch 2002) edited by Dewi Roberts
The Forward Book of Poetry 1998 edited by John Fuller
In The Criminal's Cabinet. (nthposition press 2004) edited by Val Stevenson & Todd Swift
Intimate Portraits (Seren 1995) edited by Alison Lloyd
Mooving Wails / Mit Muvelsz (Budapest 2000) edited by Kinga Kovacs
New British Poetry (Paladin 1988) edited by Gillian Allnutt, Fred D'Aguiar, Ken Edwards and Eric Mottram
Over Milk Wood (2000) edited by Peter Read & Sally Roberts Jones
The Poetry of Pembrokeshire (Seren 1989) edited by Tony Curtis
Poetry Wales Twenty Five Years (Seren 1990) edited by Cary Archard
Poetry Wales Forty Years (Seren 2005) edited by Robert Minhinnick
Short Fuse (Rattaplax 2002) edited by Phil Horton & Todd Swift
Twentieth Century Anglo-Welsh Poetry (Seren Books) edited by Dannie Abse
Wales In Our Own Image (Gwenda Williams 1999) edited by Gwenda Williams
Word Score Utterance Choreography (Writers Forum 1998) edited by Bob Cobbing & Lawrence Upton
Balloon was used as part of the Llathyard Bus Shelter Poster Project (1998)
Facing The Flowers was illustrated by Chan Ky-Yut and published in a limited edition by Lyric Editions in 2004
The River appeared on Poetry In Performance Vol One, a CD from 57 Productions (2002)
The Tao of Dining appeared in the 2005 edition of *The Good Food Guide*

For details of original magazine publication see the original collections.

The Author

Peter Finch is a poet, critic, author and literary entrepreneur living in Cardiff, Wales. He is Chief Executive of Academi, the Welsh National Literature Promotion Agency and Society of Writers. As a writer he works in both traditional and experimental forms. He is best known for his declamatory poetry readings, his creative work based on his native city of Cardiff and his encyclopedic knowledge of the UK poetry publishing scene.

Also by Peter Finch

Poetry
Wanted For Writing Poetry (with Steve Morris) – Second Aeon, 1968
Pieces Of The Universe – Second Aeon, 1969
Cycle Of the Suns – Art Living, 1970
Beyond The Silence – Vertigo, 1970
An Alteration In The Way I Breathe – Quickest way Out, 1970
The Edge Of Tomorrow (with Jeanne Rushton) – BB Books, 1971
The End Of The Vision – (hard and paper editions) - John Jones Ltd, 1971
Whitesung – Aquila, 1972
Antarktika – Writers Forum, 1972
Trowch Eich Radio 'Mlaen – Writers Forum, 1977
Connecting Tubes – Writers Forum, 1980
Visual Texts 1970-1980 – (microfiche edition) Pyrofiche, 1981
The O Poems – Writers Forum, 1981
Blues And Heartbreakers – Galloping Dog, 1981
Some Music And A Little War – Rivelin Grapheme, 1984
On Criticism – Writers Forum, 1984
Reds In The Bed – Galloping Dog, 1985
Selected Poems – Poetry Wales Press, 1987
Make – Galloping Dog, 1990
Cheng Man Ch'ing Variations – Writers Forum, 1990
Poems For Ghosts – Seren Books, 1991
Five Hundred Cobbings – Writers Forum, 1994
The Spe ell – Writers Forum, 1995
Useful – Seren Books, 1997
Dauber – Writers Forum, 1997
Antibodies – Stride, 1997
Food – Seren Books, 2001
Vizet – *Water* – Konkret Konyvek, 2003

The Welsh Poems – Shearsman, 2006
Selected Later Poems – Seren (2007)
Zen Cymru – Seren (due 2009)

Recordings
Big Band Dance Music – Balsam Flex, 1980
Dances Interdites – Balsam Flex, 1982
The Italian Job (with Bob Cobbing) – Klinker Soundz, 1985

Other Works
Blats – Second Aeon, 1973
Between 35 And 42 – Alun Books, 1982
Getting Your Poetry Published (15 editions) – Association of Little Presses, 1973
Publishing Yourself, Not Too Difficult After All (8 editions) – Association of Little Presses, 1989
How To Publish Your Poetry (3 editions) – Allison & Busby, 1985
How To Publish Your Poetry (complete revision) Read a sample chapter – Allison & Busby, April, 1998
How To Publish Yourself (two editions) – Allison & Busby, 1987
How To Publish Yourself (complete revision) Read a sample chapter – Allison & Busby, December 1997
The Poetry Business – Seren, 1994
Real Cardiff - Seren – 2002
Real Cardiff #2 – Seren, 2004
Real Wales – Seren (due 2008)

As Editor
Typewriter Poems – Something Else Press, 1972
How To Learn Welsh – Christopher Davies 1978
Green Horse (with Meic Stephens) – Christopher Davies, 1978
Small Presses & Little Magazine Of The UK & Ireland, An Address List – Oriel Bookshop, 1996
The Big Book of Cardiff (with Grahame Davies) – Seren 2005

Series Editor
For Seren Books: The Real Wales series. *Real Newport* (Ann Drysdale). Coming soon *Real Swansea* (Nigel Jenkins), *Real Wrexham* (Grahame Davies), *Real Aberystwyth* (Niall Griffiths), *Real Merthyr* (Mario Basini), and *Real Liverpool* (Niall Griffiths)